THE TWENTY EIGHT

THE TWENTY EIGHT

Living with the aftershocks. Stories from survivors and family members
of those who perished in the 1959 Yellowstone Earthquake.

ANITA PAINTER THON

ISBN: 1505453518
ISBN 13: 9781505453515

To the twenty-eight people who were taken from us, rest in peace, and know that you are not forgotten. The family and friends you left behind love and miss you dearly. We long to see you once again. May God bless you and keep you in his loving arms until then.

Be still, my soul: The Lord is on thy side;
With patience bear thy cross of grief or pain.
Leave to thy God to order and provide;
In every change he faithful will remain.
Be still, my soul: Thy best, thy heavenly Friend
Thru thorny ways leads to a joyful end.

Be still, my soul: The hour is hastening on
When we shall be forever with the Lord,
When disappointment, grief, and fear are gone,
Sorrow forgot, love purest joys restored.
Be still, my soul: When change and tears are past,
All safe and blessed we shall meet at last.

(Katharine Von Schlegel, "Favorite Christian Hymn")

Contents

Acknowledgments

I WOULD LIKE TO thank my husband, Steve, and my children, Ryan, Trish, Zach, and Danielle, for the encouragement and support they have given me in writing the story about the 28 victims of the Yellowstone (Hebgen Lake) earthquake. This is also for the 150 people who were injured and other survivors who were affected by this terrible earthquake.

Thank you to my friend Jose Munoz for his encouragement and expertise in genealogy. He sparked a fire within me to keep searching and not to give up when I faced many leads that turned cold.

To the family members of the victims—Wallace Edgerton, Joyce Elgaard, Janice M. Booth, Helen Miller, Diana Zylicz, Cicely Ballard San Filippo, and Clio Bonnett—I'm forever grateful that I was able to meet you, if only through e-mail and phone. You were so gracious and kind to share information about your loved ones. It was such a heartbreaking time that forever changed all of our lives. I now have a glimpse of the twenty-eight people.

I have found they were precious in every way!

Thanks to Joanne Girven from the beautiful Earthquake Lake Visitor Center, the US Forest Service, and the Yellowstone Association for your support.

The Twenty-Eight

MY NAME IS Anita Painter Thon. I'm a survivor of the West Yellowstone earthquake of 1959. In July 2014, I wrote my first book, *Shaken in the Night*. It is a story about the Painter family of five—my family—and how our lives were changed forever the night of August 17, 1959.

Let's take a trip to West Yellowstone. As you drive six miles down the Madison River Canyon from West Yellowstone, you will come upon Quake Lake, which was created when the landslide from the 7.5 magnitude Yellowstone earthquake blocked the flow of the Madison River. Looking toward the mountain range, you can see the huge slide area. This is where the slide spread debris three hundred feet deep across the canyon, creating a small mountain on the other side.

Geologists have said that the debris field was mostly rock, which crushed everything in its path. During the earthquake, the rock buttress high up on the almost eight-thousand-foot mountain broke loose. This caused the mountain to split in two, sending boulders, rocks, and pine trees down into the canyon. This included a house-sized boulder, which rode the debris like a surfer on a surfboard—geologists say that the lichens were still on the huge boulder, which indicated to them that it never rolled down the mountain. The sound that night was deafening.

Large boulders broke loose from the buttress.

The Earthquake Lake Visitor Center is perched on the debris field, which overlooks the huge slide. The center was remodeled and reopened to the public on Memorial Day 2014. It is a beautiful memorial to the victims who perished there. Time has passed, and the land is healing, softening the scars the earthquake left. But the memories still remain etched in many hearts.

Each time I come to West Yellowstone to visit the Earthquake Lake Visitor Center, I always take a walk up the hill to look at the Memorial Boulder, which holds the names of the twenty-eight victims of the earthquake. On the bronze plaque, I see my mother's name and feel sad and cheated that I didn't get to share my life with her.

As I look at the list of names on the memorial plaque, I think about how saddening it is that entire families were wiped out by the slide in a matter of minutes. Nine little children lost their lives that night, with their ages ranging from eighteen months to fifteen years old. Two children were orphaned after losing their parents in the earthquake. This was a horrible ordeal. Most survivors and families of the victims still live with the nightmare of losing their loved ones in such a horrible way.

Most of the people that I have met and talked to at the Earthquake Lake Visitor Center tell me that the place seems really eerie, and they feel afraid just being there. I can understand why they would feel that way; they are probably trying to visualize what happened there that night. But for me now, I seem to be drawn to West Yellowstone to see the earthquake slide. I can't really explain how I feel about being there; it is surreal as I look at the place where I cheated death. My life was spared for a reason, and I feel like I should do what I can to honor the victims.

It's holy ground now, as far as I'm concerned, for those precious lives that still lie there. When I come through the doors of the visitor center, I can feel their presence. From what I have observed with the visitors who come there, they seem to be very quiet and respectful. Some are teary-eyed. I like to think that maybe they can feel their presence too.

As time has passed, I have had a strong desire to know more about these wonderful families. Who were these people? I want the world to know about them, that they lived and their lives counted. I have been researching family history sites trying to gain any information I could find. I wish I had started searching years ago, because I'm finding a lot of their relatives have already passed on.

When I'm standing at the lookout at the visitor center and looking across to the massive slide, I try to picture where the Rock Creek campground would have been. I have heard that if you look out about one hundred yards toward the slide, you can visualize where it is. The campground was mostly buried by the slide, and the remaining area is underwater. It's a ghostly sight to see the pines sticking out of the water; it is a haunting reminder to me to see the place where we once camped. The main slide is still exposed after nearly fifty-six years, and nothing seems to grow there. I think maybe it stays that way so we don't forget what happened. It's amazing to think that our family's car and trailer are still under the water, and I've wondered what it must look like now. The film shown at the Earthquake Lake Visitor Center hypothesizes that in time the lake will go away and the Madison River will continue to flow through the canyon, maybe exposing everything that was covered that night. I know there must be other cars and trailers under the water as well as ours.

* * *

James Robertson, an excavating contractor from Great Falls, Montana, who was working at the slide area, wrote an article titled "Did Some Awesome Explosion Trigger Big Madison Quake?" With his expertise in excavating, he had a theory about the earthquake and what caused the mountain to break apart and tumble down. He states, "There must have been a terrific blast—a blast so big it is impossible to believe" that sent the side of the mountain across the Madison Canyon in southwestern Montana. He based his theory on several facts. All bodies recovered from the slide were nude, indicating that their clothing was blown off. The trees were lying with their roots pointing up the mountain, and much of the rock at the top of the slide is quartzite, which geologists claim was below the bed of the Madison River before the quake.

He believed the action that touched off the slide came in three stages, each taking a matter of minutes. First, he theorized that a terrific explosion occurred below the river, blowing the quartzite and trees several hundred feet up the mountainside and taking the "toe" out of the mountain. This caused the slide that rolled over Rock Creek campground and dammed the river. Finally, the quake itself followed and pushed many of the rocks up the mountain.

The slide at Rock Creek campground with the quake lake forming

Jolt Jars University
Needle Off Scale

GROUND VIBRATIONS FROM the Montana earthquake hit the University of Utah seismograph with such violence that the instrument was thrown "off scale" for four minutes. Dr. Kenneth L. Cook, head of the department of geophysics, estimated the magnitude of the initial shock recorded at 11:38 p.m. Monday at between 7 and 8 on the Richter scale. This rolled over the Rock Creek campground and pushed many rocks up the mountains.

Although magnitude measurements of the 1959 earthquake vary, the University of Utah recorded the quake at both 7.3 and 7.5 on the Richter scale. While other seismographs recorded the quake at 7.8, the 1959 earthquake is comparable to the 1906 San Francisco earthquake as one of the strongest earthquakes in North America, behind the 1964 magnitude 9.2 Good Friday earthquake in Alaska. The 1959 earthquake is also the most severe earthquake in the Rocky Mountain area of the United States.

The results of the quake left minor damage throughout southern Montana, northeast Idaho, and northwest Wyoming. It was felt as far as Seattle, Washington, to the west, Banff, Canada, to the north, Dickinson, North Dakota, to the east, and Provo, Utah, to the south. This area includes nine western states and three Canadian provinces. Aftershocks continued for several months.

At first, it was reported that the number of persons who died in the cracking earthquake and landslides that followed probably would never be known, and that it would be days, weeks, and months before the total number of missing could be determined and possibly days before the canyon area and lake could be thoroughly searched.

* * *

Many friends from my hometown of Ogden, Utah, have told me they had family members who were in the Yellowstone area at the time of the earthquake. For days, they did not hear from them and feared that they had been affected by the quake or possibly killed. They were relieved to finally hear the good news that their families were safe and well. They soon returned home with all kinds of stories about what they had felt or seen, so thankful they were not in an area of destruction. Others spoke of having premonitions that made them pack up and leave the area earlier because they felt uneasy being there, as my mother did. Our problem was we didn't leave like the others did.

Many campers left the Rock Creek campground Sunday night. News and forest service reports indicate that the death toll would have been a lot higher had the quake happened on the weekend when the canyon was completely full of campers. I think about those people who left earlier. How shocked but relieved they must have been when they heard about the earthquake the next day and realized just how fortunate they were to have left when they did—especially those people who might have been camping at the point where most of the deaths occurred.

Stories of Terror

I CAME ACROSS THIS story from the *Montana Standard* about a caretaker of the Hebgen Dam the night of the earthquake.

The caretaker at Hebgen Dam, George Hungerford, and his wife Ruth, were awakened by a series of explosions at 11:35 p.m. At first he thought the Russians were bombing the dam less than half a mile up the Madison River from their home.

George Hungerford and Lester Caraway, his assistant, finally recognized it was an earthquake and with their wives, they hurried to a water gage downstream from the dam to see if the river flow showed that the dam was leaking. As they neared the gage, Hungerford heard a roar. He glanced up to see a wave of water about four feet high moving down the river. Fearing that this meant the collapse of the dam, he returned to his house on the highway above the gage and tried to telephone a warning, but the line was dead. The two couples then drove toward high ground near the dam and arrived there about 11:55 p.m.

A cloud of red dust blotted out the moon, turning the night dark. The water had withdrawn from sight, but they noticed that the downstream side of the dam was wet. Then before they could see it, they heard water again; it was coming down the lake. They climbed out of the way and watched water rise, over topping the dam by three feet. After five or ten minutes, it receded, and then the wave disappeared from sight. "All we could see down the dam was darkness again."

The crest of the dam was again submerged in ten to fifteen minutes, but this time by less water, and the water receded sooner. In all there were four surges over the crest.

Many of the campers downstream from the dam were slow to realize what had happened. They woke up and looked about them, confused, but the aftershocks alerted most of them to the danger. They abandoned their trailers and fled by car to higher ground.

At Rock Creek campground hurricane force winds blew, accompanied by a surge of water one hundred feet up the mountain. Trees crashed, rocks and debris flew through the air like missiles as the mountain began tumbling down. Cries for help and screams and moans of the injured and dying rent the stillness. Naked and partially clothed people, caked with mud, or bloody in some cases, were blown, washed and flung about, and hunted frantically for survivors.

So began the disastrous night that resulted in twenty-eight officially known dead, 150 injured (fifty critically), the formation of Quake Lake, and the trapping of about 350 people in the Madison River Canyon for ten hours.

* * *

Reporter Jerry Voros wrote in the *Salt Lake Tribune* on August 19, 1959:

I walked in the valley of death Wednesday. That's the name that generation of Americans will call the six-and-a-half-mile-long, winding canyon, which took numerous lives on August 17, 1959.

Call it the valley of the brave, of the earthquake, of the dead.

For surely this was the place that at least eight persons met their death.

It was a green Wednesday. At first, entering the canyon below the dam site, the only thing strange was the lack of noise and the muddy brown river. Usually, the Madison River winds its way in a crystal clear path through the valley.

But not that Wednesday.

Mud and debris of all types floated gently downstream. And closer to the end of the canyon and the huge fifty-five-million-ton-rock slide which closed the valley—the water gets dirtier and the stream bed gets wider.

Here it is twice the normal size. It's about 2.5 times wider. Then about a turn in the road, one grabs for support.

Transfigured from a peaceful camping area into a scene of utter and complete destruction, the valley (or is it a canyon) stops.

Yes, stops!

This is a dead end.

$$* * *$$

I found the following article published in the *Montana Standard*, dated Tuesday, August 25, 1959. It explains how the earthquake had impacted tourism in Yellowstone. It also contains a prediction of how it could increase the number of visitors in the future, making it one of the top attractions in the world. In 2014, the park hosted 3,513,484 visitors.

EARTHQUAKE LAKE TO BE MAJOR ATTRACTION

Biggest Landslide in the World

Curiosity-seekers are barred from the Madison Canyon quake area for the time being. But we freely predict that it will become one of the nation's foremost tourist attractions once order is restored. On display will be a dam of major proportions, which was built in the flutter of an eyelid. It will be the strangest of all dams. Most likely it is the last resting place of unnumbered persons.

A lake which will be about one-third the size of Hebgen Dam, just above it, is being formed. It is estimated the new lake will hold about one hundred thousand acre feet of water. Its greatest depth will be about 150 feet. It will be about seven miles long. The dam itself is of enormous proportions. It stretches 4,400 feet along the bed of the Madison River. It is almost exactly a mile wide in the other direction.

It is estimated that about ninety million tons of material including earth, rocks, and trees swept down into the Madison valley when an earthquake rocked the area a week ago. In its path was a popular camping area, and in the camp were an unknown number of people. Perhaps the exact number will forever remain a mystery.

A major road repair job will have to be done in the area.

The roads for miles around will have to be entirely rebuilt. They may also have to be entirely rerouted. Perhaps the work will have to wait until it is established that this series of quakes have subsided. When a repair job was started inside Yellowstone Park, a group of workmen narrowly missed being caught in another landslide set in motion by a temblor.

This was one major disaster that did not immediately attract the curious. Instead, it repelled them. Yellowstone Park visitors immediately slumped from an average of eighteen thousand a day to between ten and eleven thousands of visitors.

The park was well on its way to a new record when the earthquake struck. Had the attendance kept up? Superintendent Lemuel Garrison had predicted that 1,600,000 people would have passed through the park by closing time. There will be a new attraction next year, a great lake caused by a landslide. And it may turn out to have been the largest landslide of modern times, or, in other words, the largest landslide in the world. Nobody will have any sort of a claim to fame without having seen this eighth wonder of the world.

The Stowes

THIS IS STORY about a young family—parents who took the opportunity to get away, to enjoy spending time together before the end of summer. The couple had gone back to the Rock Creek campground, camping at a popular location called the Point. This spot is where Robert Stowe's brothers had come the prior week for some great fishing. Thankfully, their young son, Terry, who was three and a half years old, wasn't with his parents. As fate would have it, he was safe at home in the care of his grandparents.

The Stowes had many trials in their short lives here on earth. An infant daughter born May 9, 1957, died prematurely the same day she was born. A year later, on August 23, 1958, a son, Russell Lee, was born and died six hours after his premature birth. Sadly, twenty-four-year-old Marilyn, Terry's mother, would die on August 17, a year later.

Thomas Mark Stowe (thirty), born May 22, 1929, Murray, Utah.

Parents:
Thomas William Stowe, born May 28, 1905, Salt Lake City, Utah.
Leola Boulter Stowe, born December 2, 1908, Sandy, Utah.

Thomas graduated from Jordan High School and Brigham Young University. He attended the University of Utah for two years before receiving his degree from BYU in 1951. He served in the US Army Medical Corps from 1951 to 1953 and spent one year in Korea. He was a music teacher in the Jordan Utah school district. He supervised elementary music at Riverton, Herriman, Lark, Copperton, Bingham Central, and West Jordan elementary schools and taught in the Jordan District after his release from the service.

Siblings:
Maxine Stowe Crapo, born November 17, 1927, Murray, Utah.
Robert Arthur Stowe, born July 27, 1933, Murray, Utah.

Grandparents:
John Stowe, born March 4, 1867, Trowbridge, Wiltshire, England.
Ada Alfreda Emery, born November 29, 1871, Salt Lake City, Utah.

Mrs. Marilyn Stowe (twenty-four), born August 29, 1934, Salt Lake City, Utah.

Parents:
Rex Grange Whitmore, born 1912, Midvale, Utah.
Ferrol Smith, born 1913, Draper, Utah.

Marilyn attended schools in Salt Lake City and Phoenix, Arizona, before graduating from Jordan High School. She attended Brigham Young University for one year, where she was affiliated with the Cami Los social unit. She was a stay-at-home mother.

Siblings:
Connie Lee Whitmore Smith, date and place of birth unknown.
Kay Whitmore, born 1935, Utah.
Geraldine Whitmore Hooker, born 1938, Utah.

Grandparents:
Samuel Moroni Whitmore, born 1863, Utah.
Elizabeth Letita Grange, born 1872, Utah.

Thomas married Marilyn Whitmore on November 24, 1954, in the Salt Lake Temple of the Church of Jesus Christ of Latter-day Saints.

Children:
Terry Mark Stowe (three and a half years old at the time of his parents' death), born 1956, Murray, Utah, living in Murray at the present time.

Infant girl Stowe, born and died prematurely, May 9, 1957, Murray, Utah.

Russell Lee Stowe, born and died prematurely, August 23, 1958, Murray, Utah.

* * *

Little Boy Can't Imagine His Dad Is Dead in the Quake

From Sandy, Utah, then three and a half years old, Terry Mark Stowe went fishing with his dad on Sunday, August 16, 1959, as a reward so that his mother and father could get away together for a more extended outing on that following Monday. His parents were killed when the earthquake-shaken mountain collapsed onto a popular camping spot on the Madison River below Hebgen Dam in southwestern Montana.

At that time Terry had been staying with relatives. He was told about his father but did not realize fully what it meant. "Nothing can happen to my dad," he said. He hadn't been told about his mother yet.

The body of his father, T. Mark Stowe, was found on the downstream side of the huge slide area. Terry's mother was missing and presumed dead after she was blown underneath the slide. The Stowes' auto was one of the cars found rolled up like a wad of crumpled paper, resting only a few hundred feet away from the avalanche.

The positive identification was made on T. Mark Stowe by his brothers, Robert A. and Richard W. Stowe, and his father-in-law, Rex G. Whitmore, from Sandy, Utah. The search for Marilyn, the victim's wife, continued.

Mr. Stowe, the victim's father, reported that his son, Robert, a Salt Lake County deputy sheriff, said it "looked as if Mark was in bed at the time of the landslide from the way he was dressed…Mark was a light sleeper and Marilyn a heavy sleeper. It is possible that Mark may have heard the rumble and jumped out of the tent to see what was happening when the slide hit him and knocked him free of it," Mr. Stowe theorized.

He said that the couple left for the outing that Monday morning and had gone to a spot where Robert and Richard, Stowe's brothers, had good luck fishing about ten days prior to the quake, Mr. Stowe said. They were parked between the road and the river.

Whitmore said the two brothers, Robert and Richard, had searched the huge slide area since the earthquake in an attempt to find the woman's body. The volunteers came dressed in dungarees and equipped with shovels, picks, saws, and axes, eager to help in the search.

A bulldozer was used the Friday after the quake to push aside the crumbled rock and twisted timber at the bottom of the huge slide to help locate any victims.

Thomas M. Stowe . . . Sandy man missing, feared dead. | Mrs. Thomas Stowe . . . Reported missing with husband.

A mighty convulsion of the earth and this is all that remained of the Mark Thomas | Stowe auto, caught in a tidal wave of the Madison River and shredded and scattered.

Mr. Whitmore, Marilyn's father, arrived at the slide scene on Wednesday, August 18, the day after searchers found the body of Mark Stowe. Mr. Whitmore dug at the slide area until his hands bled and then called upon his Sandy neighbors for help. They responded magnificently.

But Saturday afternoon, his face gray with weariness, Mr. Whitmore admitted defeat. Searchers who combed the riverbed below the slide had uncovered Marilyn's sleeping bag, cooking equipment, her purse, and some clothing identified as hers. But there was no body.

"I had a feeling that if we did not find her this afternoon, it was no use." A simple, moving prayer, offered in the shadows of the eighty-five-million-ton landslide across Madison Canyon fifteen miles northwest of the slide site on Saturday, marked the end of a sorrow-choked search for the body of the twenty-four-year-old woman. About forty friends and relatives of Mrs. Marilyn Whitmore Stowe listened with bowed heads and tear-dimmed eyes as Bishop Richards, kneeling in the silent circle, offered a short and simple prayer.

"If Marilyn's body is not found," he said, "we ask thee to accept this as her final resting place." Then he offered a moving plea for God's solace for her loved ones.

"There wasn't one of us who didn't shed a tear," reported Salt Lake County Deputy Sheriff C. W. Brady, one of the jeep patrol members. Even while the searchers dug at the rocks and rubble Saturday in the hunt for the body, aftershocks of Monday's disastrous quake continued to rock the area. While men dug below, one man constantly watched a high point to the north of the canyon rim opposite the mountain that had split in half to form the slide for any further evidence of falling rocks and soil.

After the simple ceremony marked the end of the search, members of the party climbed silently into their various vehicles and drove away. Nothing more could be done. Later, formal funeral services were held for the couple in Sandy, Utah.

Photo by Larry Finnegan, Deseret News
Courtesy of the Deseret News

A circle of rescuers offers prayer.

I had an opportunity to personally meet the Stowes' son, Terry Mark Stowe, at the fiftieth reunion of the Yellowstone earthquake, which was held in 2009 in West Yellowstone. I was able to introduce myself as being a survivor of the earthquake. I shared with him that I had also lost a parent and that our family had been camped in Rock Creek campground near where his parents were. I told him it must have been so hard losing both parents at such a young age and how tragic it was for him to grow up without them. He said that he was very young when they were killed, so he doesn't really remember a lot about his life with them. After that, he had been raised by his grandparents. He told me he has had a happy life.

The Stowes were a wonderful young couple just starting out in life. They had endured many trials in their short married life, and then for them to be taken in the earthquake at Yellowstone is mind-boggling. The only way I can handle it is to imagine they are now together and all is well.

The Ballards

I HAVE SPENT MANY hours searching for living family members of the Ballards. It doesn't seem possible that one family could endure so many painful experiences in a lifetime, but they did. Even though they lost their son Michael, they pushed on to make a great life for Christopher. I believe they must have been such amazing parents. My heart is full of love and compassion for this sweet family.

Sydney D.A. Ballard (forty-five), born about 1914 in Sheppey, Kent, England.

Parents:
Thomas Albert Ballard, born 1888, Sheerness, Kent, England.
Agnes Maria Goldsmith, born 1891, Strood, Kent, England.

Sibling:
Cicely Ballard San Filippo, born April 1925, Sheppey, Kent, England, now ninety years old and living in British Columbia.

Grandparents:
William Ballard, born 1851, Bradwell, Essex, England.
Hannah Hines, born 1851, Paglesham, Essex, England.

Margaret Fielder Ballard (thirty-nine), born about 1920, Sheppey, Kent, England.

Parents:
Walter Fielder, born 1895, West Moors, Dorset, England.
Ethel Haskell, born 1895, West Moors, Dorset, England.

Sibling:
Joyce Fielder Elgaard, born 1925, Wimborne, England, living in Kelowna, British Columbia.

Grandparents:
Albert Fielder, born 1871, England.
Emma Norris, born 1873, England.

Sydney and Margaret's children:
Michael Ballard (ten), born 1942, Sheppey, Kent, England. Died 1952 in Canada.

Christopher Thomas Ballard (nine), born 1950, Canada.

The *Aquitania*

Sydney Douglas Albert Ballard married Margaret Haskell Fielder in Maidstone, Kent, England, in 1942. The family had emigrated from England from the port of Southampton to Halifax, Nova Scotia, Canada, with their son, Michael, who was four years old at the time. They came over on a ship named *Aquitania* in November 1947.

They must have been so excited for their new adventure in Canada. It is unclear whether they followed other relatives who may have emigrated with them from England.

I have been diligently searching for any living members of the Ballard family for the past two years. I was hoping to locate family members that might be related to the Ballard family. I finally got a lucky break on March 30, 2015.

I had recently found on Ancestry.com that Margaret Fielder Ballard's maiden name was Haskell. After more searching, I was able to find the people I thought could be her parents. I had a feeling that I should check the My Heritage website, just to see what I might find there. To my surprise, I found a family tree for Margaret Haskell Fielder belonging to a Janice M. Booth. I sent an e-mail right away to the owner of the family tree to see what the response would be. In the past, most of my e-mails asking about other family trees hadn't turned up any information.

When I saw the return e-mail come through the next day, I was thrilled. I couldn't wait to see what the response would be. When I read the reply from Janice Booth, I was elated to find out that she is Margaret Ballard's niece, and Joyce Elgaard is Margaret Ballard's sister. She explained that she usually spends most of her time on Ancestry.com, where she enters information, but on that day she went to the My Heritage website instead. She told me she thinks she went there instead because I was meant to find her there. I really believe that!

* * *

An Interview with Janice Booth

This is our story. Mum, Joyce Elgaard, and I were two days late coming home from Girl Guide camp in British Columbia. Margaret Ballard was my aunt, my mum's sister. There's another sister who still lives in England.

We were on our way to pick up my brother and sister, who were staying with cousins in Alberta before heading to West Yellowstone. We were a day late in meeting up at Yellowstone with the Ballards, which would have put us there at the time of the earthquake.

On the way, we heard a radio report that the Ballard family from British Columbia had been killed in an earthquake in the northwest. Mum phoned the police, who were really helpful, and found out what was going on. We did go on to Yellowstone, and I guess left contact information, because Mum later received a letter from the Bennett family.

The Bennett family had written Joyce a letter, introducing themselves and letting her know that while staying at the Rock Creek campground, they had befriended the Ballards. They told Joyce of the horror they experienced of watching the slide come down and engulf the Ballards' car. There was no way they could have escaped, because it happened so quickly. The Bennetts almost perished as it was, and although injured, they were able to get to higher ground. They were hospitalized because of their injuries and shock.

Prior to meeting Janice, I had traced the Ballard family to Vancouver, British Columbia, where I was able to locate a voting record from 1953. I tried without any luck to find photos so that I could see the family I had envisioned in my mind. From there, I found that they had moved to Nelson, British Columbia, a city located in the Selkirk Mountains on the extreme western arm of Kootenay Lake. The town built its own hydro-electric generating system, which is on the waterway. It seemed logical that Sydney would be working and living there, since he was a marine engineer.

As I uncovered details about the family, my heart became heavy with the unfortunate facts that I found about them.

The Ballards had two sons with major health problems. The oldest son, Michael, was ten when he became ill with pneumonia. He was taken to the children's hospital in Vancouver, where he passed away on Christmas Day, 1952. This left the couple with one son, Christopher Thomas, who was two at the time of Michael's death. Christopher was crippled and confined to a wheelchair. Both boys had muscular dystrophy. Learning about the Ballards' children both being afflicted with serious health problems was very distressing. The family had met with so many trials at every turn. It's unfathomable with everything they had been through that they would perish together in an earthquake seven years later while on a holiday to Yellowstone. It brings me peace to imagine that they are together with Michael once again. Safe, secure, and happy!

* * *

West Yellowstone, Montana (AP)

A Red Cross official said today it appears that three Canadians can be presumed dead in the Montana earthquake. They are Mr. and Mrs. Sydney D. Ballard and their son Christopher of Nelson, B.C.

The statement that the Ballards can be presumed dead came from Joseph Hladecek, who came from San Francisco to help set up a relief center for the victims of the earthquake.

He had talked with Ballard's mother, who went to Red Cross headquarters at Bozeman, Montana, to check on his whereabouts. Hladecek did not retain a record of her name. Hladecek is in charge of compiling the list of missing at the Bozeman office. He quoted the mother as saying there is no doubt in her mind that the Ballards were killed.

While searching the historic newspapers, I came across an article in the *Salt Lake Tribune* about the Ballard family being in the Rock Creek campground at the time of the earthquake. There are two accounts about the Ballards: one from Henry F. Bennett and another from Henry's wife. They were a family from Cottonwood, Arizona, camped next to the Ballard family.

Mr. and Mrs. Henry F. Bennett of Cottonwood, Ariz. said, "we were camped next to the Ballards from British Columbia and their nine-year-old son, a wheelchair victim. They were sleeping in their station wagon near our camp when the major mountain slide roared down after the quake, damming the Madison River. The Bennetts said they had become friendly with the Ballards and are certain the Canadian family did not escape. Says when the quake hit we heard them scream and watched as they tried to get out, but the water swept them away," Bennett said. "They're surely dead," he added.

Mr. Bennett, himself a wheelchair victim of polio, was sleeping in a tent with his wife and two children. Henry F. Bennett, 41, from Cottonwood, Ariz., who with his daughter, Jeannette, 14, was flown by helicopter to West Yellowstone for emergency treatment of injuries, described the terror of the tremor.

"We felt the earth shake and then rocks began falling all around us, surrounding our whole camping area. We managed to make it to high ground before the water from the river backed up, otherwise I'm sure we would have drowned," Mr. Bennett said. "It's nothing short of a miracle that we survived," he declared.

Arizona Daily Sun, Flagstaff, Arizona, by Ed Hunt

Mrs. Henry F. Bennett of Cottonwood, Arizona thought it was a bear shaking their tent when an earthquake hit the northwest, and took sixteen lives Monday night August 17. This was her opinion expressed today when she passed through Flagstaff with her husband Henry and two children, all on their way home after being treated in the hospital for their injuries.

"But a bear doesn't make that much noise," she said. "So I got my husband up and ran to wake up the children. The river was rising fast, and Royal, our ten-year-old, feeling a spray on his face, told me sleepily that it was raining. Jeanette, fourteen, seemed too sleepy to know what was happening.

Men from other families in the Rock Creek campground in the Madison River canyon helped get Henry Bennett to higher ground, leaving his wheelchair for the moment and carrying him in his sleeping bag. "I'm such a heavy sleeper," he said, "that I didn't know anything was happening until I zipped open the tent, and saw trees flying through the air in the moonlight, and the mountains of dirt sliding down on either side of us."

Luckily for the Cottonwood family, the campground space they were in was partially protected from the upheaving earth. One family sleeping only 150 yards away (the Ballards) in their station wagon, according to Mrs. Bennett's estimate caught the full force of the slide, which pushed it and rolled it one hundred yards. "I ran over to it and saw it was covered all except one side. I could hear moans coming from inside the car, the back end seemed to be bashed in, and I couldn't get an answer to my calls. The water was rising fast, and so I ran to the high ground to get help.

One of the men went down, but when he came back said, "he couldn't hear any sound at all coming from the car. He was in waist deep water from the rising water from the Madison River backing up, when he left it.".

Sydney's mother, Agnes Goldsmith Ballard, was a widow. She had lost her husband, Thomas Albert Ballard, of a heart attack in England in 1949. After the earthquake happened, Agnes came looking for her family at the Red Cross Center in Bozeman, Montana. It was there she learned that her family might have perished after receiving information from nearby campers who witnessed the family being swept away. Agnes commented at the time that she was sure they had been killed.

She traveled back and forth from England to Canada several times on a Cunard White Star line. She did come to Canada a couple of months prior to Michael's death on October 14, 1952, possibly to help the Ballards with both of their ill sons. She traveled back and forth a couple of times after Yellowstone, eventually returning to England, where she may have lived out the rest of her life.

Cicely Ballard

Sydney did have a sister, Cicely. For a while, I couldn't locate any records that she had immigrated to Canada from England. Perhaps that is why Agnes went back and forth from Canada to England, because most of her relatives were still living in England.

A door to the past opened on May 26, 2015. I was contacted through a family history site by the granddaughter of Cicely. Her name is Clio Bonnett. She relayed the story of how her grandmother Cicely had met her grandfather Sebastian San Filippo during World War II in England, where he was stationed. She was working in a post office when they met. Sebastian was in the Royal Canadian Navy. He eventually brought Cicely to Canada, where they were married. They had a daughter, Gaye San Filippo, in 1951.

Cicely is still alive and turned ninety years old in April 2015. Clio told me that Cicely was eleven years younger than Sydney. She still speaks very fondly of him. Cicely said, "He was a great athlete and had won a lot of awards in school. He was very tall, blond, and handsome." When the war started, Sydney joined the Royal Army Service Corps in 1937, two years before the war began in 1939. He was then sent to Egypt for a five-year span of service.

Returning to England, he became an officer with the RASC, which sent him to India for another two years of service. This became a seven-year span until the war ended.

During the time Sydney spent in India, Margaret cared for their first son Michael in England. He was born with myotonia congenita, a disease that affects muscle control, leaving him unable to use his limbs.

Meanwhile, Margaret had a sister who was a nurse in Vancouver during the war. She encouraged Margaret to take Michael to see doctors at the Shriners Society. She thought they might be able to help him. But those hopes were dashed when they learned the prognosis for Michael was not good. In fact, they encouraged Margaret to have another baby as soon as possible to fill the void should they lose Michael.

When the war was over, Sydney married Margaret Fielder. He sent a letter home informing his family, which was quite a surprise to Cicely but not an unwelcome one. Shortly after the war ended, Sydney immigrated to Canada with Margaret and Michael, where they joined the rest of the Ballard family, who had also emigrated from England to Canada. Margaret and Sydney did have another baby, Christopher, who was born in Canada. As fate would have it, he was also born with the same disease as his brother Michael.

They all lived together in Ontario (Fort William and Burlington) before finally moving to Calgary, Alberta, where the rest of the family still lives today.

Clio says Cicely and her mother, Agnes Ballard, had gone to West Yellowstone after hearing about the earthquake to find out about Sydney. Unable to find any trace of the family, the women felt that it was fate, since the Ballards had arrived at the Rock Creek campground only an hour prior to the quake happening. They returned brokenhearted to inform the rest of the family of the presumed deaths of Sydney, Margaret, and Christopher.

Michael

Michael and Aunt Cicely

Christopher

Sydney and Cicely

Margaret, Michael, Sydney
and Agnes Ballard

Cicely and daughter Gia Bonnett

How tragic it is to see the names of Sydney, Margaret, and Christopher on the memorial plaque. They have not been forgotten for a moment. Their extended family members cherish and love them dearly. They have great memories of their time spent together and are doing what they can to keep their memory alive for generations to come.

The Provosts

THE PROVOST FAMILY had gone on a vacation to West Yellowstone to spend time with Richard Provost, Roger's son from a previous marriage. He was spending part of the summer with his father, stepmother Marian (Elizabeth), and his eighteen-month-old little brother, David. By all accounts from the postcards they had sent, it seemed as if they were having a great adventure, until they all perished when the earthquake slide engulfed their camp.

Roger Crow Provost (forty-three), born March 24, 1916, Dubuque, Iowa.

Parents:
P. Albert Provost, born 1879, Nebraska.
Katherine C. Tanner, born 1882, Nebraska.

Siblings:
Mary K. Provost, born 1910, Idaho.
Dorothy L. Provost, born 1915, Idaho.
Barbara Jane Provost, born 1912, Idaho.

Marian (Elizabeth) Findlay Provost (thirty-one), born May 20, 1928, Dubuque, Iowa.

Parents:
Marion Elmer Findlay, born 1892, Stanwood, Cedar, Iowa.
Margaret Ruth Davidson, born 1892, Stanwood, Cedar, Iowa.

Siblings:
Phillip Roland, born 1916, Iowa.
Margaret Louise, born 1918, Iowa.
Stanley Keith, born 1918, Iowa.
Lori Ann, born 1926, Iowa.

Richard Roger Provost (fifteen), born June 27, 1944, Oakland, California.

He was the son of Roger and Rosalyn Dayle Bussey, Roger's first wife.

Roger's second marriage was to Marian (Elizabeth) Findlay, May 28, 1955, at Carmel, Monterey, California.

David John Provost (one and a half), born April 13, 1958.
His parents are Roger and Marian (Elizabeth) Findlay Provost.

* * *

Son Given Up for Dead in Earthquake
The *San Bernardino County Sun*, September 5, 1959

A Chino woman's son and his family were believed victims of the Yellowstone National Park earthquake. They failed to return yesterday to Soledad as scheduled.

His mother, Katherine Provost, said yesterday she has been forced to conclude that her son is dead. The mother added she has heart trouble, and her son had made a point of writing her approximately every other day. He had also provided her an itinerary, so she could contact him in an emergency.

Mrs. Provost said she last heard from her son, Roger, in a card dated August 16, a day before the quake struck. "The letters stopped coming after the quake," she said, and authorities were unable to turn up other points on the itinerary.

Katherine Provost, Roger's mother, did pass away shortly after her son in 1959.

* * *

A news bulletin:

> Mr. and Mrs. Marion Findlay of Ontario, California, have notified relatives here that their daughter, Mrs. Marian (Elizabeth) Findlay Provost, thirty-one, and her husband, Roger Provost, forty-one, deputy superintendent of Soledad, California state prison, and their two sons, David, eighteen months, and Richard Roger (Dick), fifteen, are listed among the missing in the recent Yellowstone National Park earthquake.

It was reported that Roger did not report to duty the Tuesday after the earthquake. He was to have been on duty at 8:00 a.m.

The last report about them came from a trailer company in West Yellowstone, where they were vacationing. State police and rangers from Idaho and Montana had been searching for them, but with no word. Also, a postcard was received by Roger's mother, Katherine Provost, on August 16, informing her that the family was camped on the Madison River. This was a day before the earthquake. He wrote, "We are camped on the Madison River about thirty miles from Yellowstone. It's a beautiful place. Fishing is fair."

Richard Roger "Dick" Provost lived with his mother, Roselyn Bussey. He was on vacation with his little brother, David, his father, Roger, and stepmother, Marian (Elizabeth), when he was lost in the quake. The blond, blue-eyed, six-foot youth's last message came to his mother in a postcard on August 12:

> Today, we visited Yellowstone Park and Old Faithful, where we saw Old Faithful and all of the many geysers. Last night, we parked the car and trailer along the side of the road. Some rangers threw us out.
> Love, Dick.

His mother later learned that they were fishing on the Madison River, about thirty miles from West Yellowstone. They had been planning on leaving the area in the morning before the earthquake. His mother said, "But I guess they liked the fishing there too well. They never left."

Richard was in the scholarship society at Stanford Jr. High twice for good grades. He was an accomplished clarinetist and saxophone player. He was a member of the school's orchestra band and Dixieland group. He had been awarded a spot with the all-city junior orchestra. He was getting ready to start high school in the couple of days prior to his death. He was active in the Unitarian church, where he was treasurer of the church's Emerson club.

What a wonderful young man Richard Roger was. He had accomplished so many things in his short life here on earth. His little brother, David, was such a delight, so full of life, and at one and a half, he was just beginning to explore this great big world when he was tragically taken from it.

Richard Roger Provost

Sadly, the Provost family is listed on the memorial plaque. The two boys were so young, just starting out, and so full of promise. This was an amazing family that was taken too soon.

The Edgertons

MERLE AND EDNA Edgerton were friends of Harmon and Edna Woods. They were traveling together on vacation to the West Yellowstone area. They headed to the Madison River Canyon to camp at the Rock Creek campground. Both Merle and Harmon loved to fish and were looking forward to some great fishing on the Madison River at the Point, a popular spot for fisherman. Several survivors of the slide witnessed cars and trailers being crushed and buried by the massive slide. It is feared that they were caught in it and perished there together.

Edna May Noble Edgerton, born 1910, Utah.

Parents:
Lewis Burt Noble, born 1874, Iowa.
When the United States declared war on Germany in 1917, Edna M. Edgerton was probably living in Utah. In 1935, Edna was living in Pasadena, California.

Harriet May Preston, born 1881, Iowa.

Wallace W. Edgerton (son), born 1934, California.
Merle Marion Edgerton, born 1911, Missouri.

Parents:
George R. Edgerton, born 1885, Ohio.
Lucy E. Perryman Edgerton, born 1880, Missouri.

Grandparents:
Jeptha Edgerton, born December 15, 1851, Athens, Ohio.
Alameda Edgerton, born 1857, Ohio.

Siblings:
Louise C. Edgerton, born 1924, Missouri.
Nola M. Edgerton, born 1915, Missouri.
Bernard W. Edgerton, born 1933, Missouri.
Ansel E. Edgerton, born 1913, Missouri.

In the 1920s, at age nine, Merle was living in Union City, Missouri, about the time that the Mississippi River flooded, forcing thousands to leave their homes.

Merle moved from Missouri to California in the 1930s, one of millions of Americans who left the Great Plains and settled elsewhere during the Dust Bowl.

Merle and Edna were married September 17, 1939, in Glendale, California. After searching for members of the Edgerton family for many months, I posted a message on Ancestry.com. Out of the blue, several weeks later, I received a reply from a lady who told me that her husband was a cousin to Merle's son, Wallace. She had his phone number and told me that he lives in California.

I was so thrilled to finally locate a family member of the Edgertons. I was apprehensive to call him at first. I was worried that he would not be receptive to my call. After all, it was fifty-five years after the earthquake.

When I called, I think it shocked him at first. I then explained that in 1959, I was in the Yellowstone earthquake. My family and I were camped in Rock Creek, the same campground as his parents. His first words were, "How old are you?" I laughed and told him I was a young child at the time of the earthquake. We had a heartfelt talk about his family. Wallace told me that he was in a barbershop getting a haircut when a news bulletin came across the radio reporting that there had been a huge earthquake in the northwest. He said his heart sank, and he immediately had a feeling that his parents were in the earthquake. He said he went home and got into his parents' bed to wait for a call that they were OK. He could not lose the feeling that they were gone. They were to leave West Yellowstone that morning and drive to his aunt's house. They never called or showed up that day, so he knew his worst fears were true.

Wallace said he was an only child and that his parents were his best friends. After their deaths, he became very distraught and started drinking. His life was in turmoil for several years. He decided that he had to make a change to turn his life around; he could not go on living like he was. He enrolled in school and went on to become a successful businessman and teacher. He became a professor in the Political Science department at Mt. San Jacinto College. He served on the Long Beach city council for seventeen years and was the former mayor of Menifee, California. Wallace is father to three daughters, DeLynn, Ally, and Toyan. He is married to Judee.

I told Wallace that his parents were probably looking down and must be so proud of his accomplishments.

Wallace had lung transplant surgery several years ago. He had been doing very well until recently, when his body started showing signs of rejection.

An e-mail I received from Wallace on September 21, 2014:

I go to surgery early tomorrow morning. Please wish me well. We, Judee and I, have sent you some photographs, which you may have already received, or will in the next couple of days. The photos are of my parents (Merle and Edna Edgerton). One of the photos was of me shaking my dad's hand (about the **eigh**th grade) the day of my dad's graduation from the University of Southern California. I was my father's only child, and Edna was unable to have children of her own and raised me from the time I was four years old; she was my mother.

The other photos include one of my dad's graduation pictures (that one might be from medical school, USC). Another photo shows my dad and my mother with my dad's ranch partner after he was in medical practice. My dad is very tan in a suit next to my mom, and on the other side is his ranch partner (the guy with the cigar).

The photo would have been taken within a couple of years or sooner of the earthquake. All the ladies lined up in a row include my mother. She worked, among other jobs, at See's Candies to help put my father through school.

When I was a child we lived in an affluent neighborhood in Southern California (Pacific Palisades), and my father was a successful salesperson. He worked for the Edison Company. About 1942, soon after WWII began, my father decided to become a medical doctor. He was thirty-three years old and only had a year and a half of community college, where he had played baseball. My mother was very supportive of this quest and would work sometimes six days a week, ten hours a day to make my father's dream come true. However, this meant we would move from our affluent neighborhood to a converted garage in El Monte, California; it was a poverty area.

Concurrently, my mother was the most loving, supportive, and caring mother to me, but as you can imagine, I saw little of them, even though they tried their best to meet my every need in a tough neighborhood. This meant my dad had to finish college, go to medical school, having a year of internship and a two-year resident in general medicine and surgery. He began his first year of his own medical practice my first year of community college. They bought a home and we began a new life in Coalinga, California.

My mother would call my dad Dr. Robin Hood because of all the free time he gave to the elderly, the poor Hispanic community, college kids, and the prison. Nevertheless, my father was a very successful medical doctor both because of a proclivity for the profession and a sense of caring for those who were without. Perhaps he gained that empathy for those who had less because of his parents (my grandparents) losing their farm in the Great Depression. He was still in school at the time.

Seven years after beginning his medical practice, my father and mother were killed in the Yellowstone earthquake. I was devastated, as were the elderly poor people in Coalinga, because the other doctors would not take their welfare checks (or treat them for free), and they would now need to travel over fifty miles to Fresno to get treatment. I might have been able to deal with my personal loss, but the loss of medical security for all those poor people made no sense to me—and still does not. I have had many quite talks with God about this event since 1959 but never in a church. I am always alone on a hilltop or a quiet forest. If there is a reason, it is beyond my comprehension, but I feel no bitterness. The wonder of the universe lets me know there is some kind of plan far beyond my ability to understand, and I surrender to that greater wisdom.

My dear Anita, we have never met but we share this tragedy, and it is wonderful that you are writing your book about this event. You are a childhood survivor of the event and lost some of your heart in this earthquake. I send you my warmest wishes and will be happy to add more information as time permits. Of course, tomorrow I face surgery and none of us know our time.

Merle and Wallace

Merle (on the left) and Edna

Edna (second from the left)

The Woodses

Harmon E. Woods (fifty-nine), born 1900, Aurora, Lawrence, Missouri.

Parents:
Henry J. Woods, born 1880, Aurora City, Lawrence, Missouri.
Nettie J. Veal, born 1879, Kentucky.

Grandparents:
Harmon Woods, born 1857, Illinois.
Nannie Woods, born 1859, Missouri.

Edna Maude Calkins Woods (fifty-five), born 1904, Missouri.

Parents:
John R. Calkins, born in England.
Mary J. Ollie, born in England.

Harmon E. and Edna Maude Woods were married July 3, 1928, in Los Angeles, California. Harmon enlisted in the army on December 4, 1942. He was a private in World War II from 1938 to 1946.

In 1930, they lived at Kern County, California. In 1940, they lived at Coalinga, Fresno County, California. City directories show them living in Fresno, California, between 1944 and 1949.

Children:

Russell Floyd Woods, born 1924 in Oklahoma. He was Edna and Harmon's only child. He was thirty-five years old at the time of his parents' death in the earthquake. Unfortunately, I wasn't able to locate him or make contact with any family he might have had. The only information I have is that he was married for a short time and then divorced. He would be about ninety-one years old today.

THE WOODS ALSO took under their wing and cared for another person, a young high school girl by the name of Otta Mae Clark. She lived with a custodial aunt that the Woods knew. Otta didn't have the best home life growing up; she had come home late from a school dance one night, causing a falling-out with her aunt. After that night, Edna took Otta into her care and provided the stable home life she needed. Edna and Harmon Woods were very compassionate, kind people and always serving others.

When Otta's mother, Opal Clark, died in June of 1947, Edna Woods drove Otta to Chelsea, Oklahoma, for the funeral. A month later, Otta married Robert Rodman in Bentonville, Arkansas. They later had three children, Diana, Robert, and Thomas (Tommie).

* * *

An Interview with Otta's Daughter, Diana

In May 1951, Edna came to visit us in Big Spring, Texas. My brother, Bobby Rodman, was a newborn. I believe Edna came to help Momma and Daddy with the family. I was sixteen months old. I'm sure that was a godsend for my parents with two children in diapers! I don't know if she came in 1954, when Tommy was born, or in 1949, when I was born. My dad was real sick with rheumatic fever in the midfifties. I can't remember whether they came to help.

My brothers, Bobby and Tommy, and I called them Grandma and Grandpa Woods. We thought they were Momma's real parents for a long time. They loved us like their own grandchildren. Edna sent us Easter outfits every year.

Harmon was employed by Shell Oil. Momma said he was a geologist, and census records list him as a pumper/oil worker. His hobby was collecting and polishing rocks. He used many of his beautiful stones to make jewelry. I still have the bracelet he made for me and the stone from a bolo tie he sent Daddy.

The 1940 census reported Edna as being a housewife, but a newspaper article in the *Coalinga Record* from August 27, 1959, says Edna was a postal carrier.

In the summer of 1958, Edna flew to Lubbock, Texas, to visit us. I remember driving there (about one hundred miles) to pick her up. On the drive back home to Big Spring, she pulled a joke on me. She said, "Railroad crossing, look out for the cars. Can you spell that without any *r*'s?" She got the biggest kick out of me concentrating hard as I said, "A-I-L-O..." I don't remember how far she let me spell before she told me the answer to the riddle was T-H-A-T!

During that visit, Grandma Woods played dolls with me. My favorite was a Ginny doll. Edna had hand-stitched a blue gingham dress and bonnet for Ginny.

She embroidered a monogram *G* on the dress pocket and on the back of the bonnet. I didn't know this was the last time I'd ever see Grandma Woods.

That next summer in 1959, the Woods family invited us to travel to Yellowstone National Park to meet them in August. They planned to camp and fish. They knew Daddy loved to fish. There were probably several reasons we didn't go: it was a long way to drive, we might not have had the money to go, school would be starting soon, and Momma was probably still sewing my new clothes for the year. Daddy might not have had any vacation time left. Was it fate that we didn't go?

One day when we got home from school, Momma told us Grandma and Grandpa Woods had been killed in the Yellowstone Earthquake. It must have been very early in the school year, because school didn't start until after Labor Day back then, and the Woods were declared dead by the court on September 3, 1959.

I don't know who notified Momma. I remember going out our back door and sitting in a flowerbed. I sat there crying and hugging our dog. Harmon and Edna Woods were special people to my family. Even though we weren't related, they treated us like their children and grandchildren. Their kindness to my mother and the support they gave her will always be remembered.

* * *

Superior Court Recognizes Coalinga's Victims from Montana Quake as Deceased

The Coalinga victims to the recent Montana earthquake disaster, Dr. and Mrs. Merle Edgerton and Mr. And Mrs. Harmon E. Woods, have been officially added to the list of the death toll in Montana.

Tuesday in Fresno, Wallace Edgerton, son of the physician and his wife, appeared with his attorney, Ted Frame, in the superior court, where he was appointed special administrator of his father's estate. The court, from the evidence and reports submitted which specified the cause and time of death, recognized Dr. Merle and Edna Edgerton as deceased. Messages from Edgerton and Woods prior to the disaster indicated that they were to go on a fishing trip on the Madison River, which was the scene of the earthquake. **Quake Probable Dead Now Is Set at 28**

Bozeman (AP) The probable toil of Montana's Yellowstone Madison Canyon earthquakes was placed at 28 Monday by the Gallatin County sheriff Donald J. Skerritt.

He stated the latest to be added to the List were Dr. Merle Edgerton and his wife Edna, of Coalinga, California and Harmon E. Woods, and his wife Edna who were also from Coalinga, California.

The names of Harmon and Edna Woods are on the Memorial Boulder as being lost in the quake. We know them as being a wonderful, loving couple taken too soon. They were always trying to serve others, as did their friends Merle and Edna, the Edgertons. Their memory still lives on through the many friends and family they have.

Myrtle Oram Painter

MY MOTHER WAS born on November 6, 1916, and grew up in Liberty, a small community in Northern Utah. Her father died of diabetes at thirty-three when she was just a small child. When he died, her mother was left alone to raise four little children. Her mother had heard of a man in town who had lost his wife due to a sudden illness. He was left alone to raise several small children as well, so they got together, courted, and eventually were married. Four more children were added to their brood. They were a very large, loving, and close family.

My mother and father, Norman (Ray), were married November 16, 1936, in Nephi, Juab County, Utah. They had four children. Twins Anita and Anne were twelve, Carole was sixteen, and Kenneth was nineteen at the time of Mother's death. My mother was devoted to her children. She was a seamstress and sewed lovely things for my sisters and me. We always had the latest fashions. She went without so that we could have the best things. She made the holidays so special.

We always took vacations together as a family and were able to see most of the western United States, Canada, and British Columbia in my twelve short years with her. I think it was important to my parents for their children to see and learn about this great country we live in. Now a mother and grandmother myself, I feel it is important for my family to do the same. Those were cherished times with my parents.

My mother worked at American Food Store, where she became the manager of the bakery. She was loved and respected by her coworkers and had many friends. After Pearl Harbor was attacked, she worked at the Defense Depot Ogden (DDO), an ammunition manufacturing plant. During her time at DDO, she earned and saved her war bonds. With these bonds, we were able to build a new, beautiful home in South Ogden, Utah. This was in the 1950s. It was sad that mother wasn't able to really enjoy the house that she worked and saved for, since she died in the earthquake shortly after it was built. Our father worked at Hill Air Force Base as a mechanic on the airplanes called the Flying Tigers.

My mother adored children, and she would have been thrilled to know that she was a grandmother of nine and a great-grandmother of twenty.

Children:

Kenneth Ray Painter, born September 21, 1939, Utah.
Carole Jean Painter, born May 13, 1943, Ogden, Utah.
Anita Mae Painter Thon, born August 7, 1947, Ogden, Utah.
Anne Marie Painter Kirkman, born August 7, 1947, Ogden, Utah.

Parents:
Elizabeth Melvina Knighton Oram Jolley, born 1889, Utah.
William Hughes Oram, born 1889, Ogden, Utah.

Siblings:
Mary Eliza Oram, born January 20, 1914.
Afton Vaughn Jolley, born March 1, 1927.
Norma Lee Jolley, born January 21, 1933.
Alice Jolley, born August 12, 1927.
Ellis Hughes Oram, born August 12, 1918.
George Willis "Bill" Oram, born April 1920.

Melvin Knighton Jolley, born May 2, 1929.
Merlyn Knighton Jolley, born March 29, 1931.

My two sisters, Anne and Carole, and I believe our mother had a premonition of some impending doom while we were on our vacation to Yellowstone. We are still reminded of Mom's comments as we were preparing for our vacation. She couldn't shake the thought that we wouldn't be coming back home. We dismissed the notion and tried to reassure her that everything was going to be wonderful and that we would have so much fun together as a family. We had just bought a beautiful twenty-five-foot trailer, and this would be our first time staying in it.

We arrived safely and spent a couple of days in the Yellowstone Park area. On the morning of August 17, the day of the earthquake, my mom felt really uneasy. To us, it appeared that she wasn't enjoying being there at all. Her only desire was to get away as far as she could from the geysers and hot pots. My dad was OK and happy with that because it would put us on the road and closer for him to be able to fish on the Madison River. As our family was walking to our car to leave the park and head for the Rock Creek campground, she said, "Let's get out of here before the whole place blows up." Little did she know that when we left there, we were heading right into peril, and her fears would be realized.

Being in the earthquake was truly a horrible experience. It was a nightmare come true—the scared-to-death, screaming, "Am I going to die?" type of nightmare. After it was over, we were amazed, shocked, and confused all at the same time. Why and how did we manage to survive while others didn't? We were thankful at first to be alive but then felt guilty that we had lived. We realized that these wonderful families we had just met hours earlier were gone, taken away in minutes, in such a tragic way.

I recently stayed at my son Zach's home in Pleasant View, Utah. I had been working on my book and had felt pretty emotional throughout the week. I had found some stories about the earthquake that brought back a lot of bad memories for me. I woke up during the night with a fright. As I looked out the large bedroom window, I could see the bright full moon, which shown down upon the mountainside near the back of his home. At that moment, in my mind's eye, I was back in West Yellowstone at the Rock Creek campground once again. I have had similar experiences of flashbacks of the sights and smells of that night. I'm not sure if that will ever completely leave me. I woke up every hour that night, it seemed, looking out at the mountain. It was as if I were waiting for something to happen, but thankfully nothing did.

I thought again about the indescribable, terrific roar. We now know that sound was a mountain three-quarters of a mile wide crashing down like a cascading waterfall, causing a hundred-mile-per-hour hurricane-force wind that pushed air, water, trees, and rocks in a massive slide toward the sleeping campers. In my book, *Shaken in the Night*, I wrote about our family's experience and how we had originally parked closer to the road when we first arrived at the Rock Creek campground. Dad wasn't completely satisfied with our camping site, so he went searching for a cooler place by the river. He did find that perfect spot, so he thought, and we moved into harm's way near the river and the mountain. I am haunted by that decision. The people that helped us after the quake were parked where we had been earlier. Was it fate?

This is what I remember happening. It was a peaceful, warm August night, our first night in Rock Creek campground in the Madison River Canyon. Mom had decided at 11:30 p.m., while the family slept, to go down and wash her hair in the Madison River near our trailer. We didn't know until later that she wasn't in the trailer with us when the earthquake struck. She was in the worst possible spot, down by the river, when the quake started.

She survived the tidal wave that swept her away, only to be thrown back into the slide. The rocks, boulders, trees, and debris from the tumbling mountain pounded her. The force crushed her chest, puncturing her lung. She also had a compound fracture of her arm, which was nearly severed at the elbow. She was thrown back out by the slide and survived being buried by only a few feet. Our trailer was about thirty feet from being completely buried and was demolished by the water, rocks, and flying trees that hit it. After it broke apart, the moonlight streamed in. We could hear the sound of dripping water after the roar and shaking had stopped. We fell out of the trailer into the cold, black water. Anne and I found that we were alone, without any knowledge of what had happened to our parents and Carole.

We frantically took turns diving under the water at the back of the trailer where our parents had slept. The trailer was smashed, and a large hole had been torn through the metal. We stuck our arms through, trying to feel for their heads. This went on for a while until we were so cold, we couldn't do it any longer. We had started to lose hope and were afraid we were going to die. We had been treading water, barely able to touch the ground, wondering if our family had been killed.

After what seemed an eternity, our older sister, Carole, finally called to us from high on a ridge that was out of the water. She told us to come quickly, that she had found Mother. After we met up with her, she told us the story of how she had found Mother downstream, which was a ways from our displaced trailer. She saw a silhouette slumped on a rock. Mother was completely naked from the terrific wind and water that had hit her. She had twigs entangled in her hair. She was bleeding profusely, which left her very weak and unable to stand without help. Carole told us, "I would have passed her by had she not called out my name." Mother had called out, "Carole, come to me. I need help."

Carole was able to see a glowing lantern hanging in a tree from a camp upon the hill, away from the rising water. It was the Green family, who themselves had barely escaped the slide. They were in their car about to leave, but they couldn't due to a pine tree being threaded underneath the car by the slide, leaving their car high-centered.

Carole approached the car with its headlights shining in her eyes. She frantically asked them not to leave. The lady she spoke with was Mildred "Tootie" Green, who thankfully was a nurse. Carole said, "Please help me! My mother has been injured by the landslide. She has lost her arm and is bleeding really badly." Tootie went to work immediately to try to stop the bleeding. Mother would have died on the spot had we headed in a different direction. I believe Tootie was truly an angel there to help the people.

As our mother's injuries were being tended to by nurse Tootie Green. Carole said, "I noticed Dad walking toward the light of the camp we are in. I ran over to him to let him know that we are all safe."

Dad said, "I saw a wall of water coming over the top of the pine trees toward me. I had only a split second to react. I could hear you girls screaming for help, but I was unable to move or even call out because of the rising water. I thought I was going to drown at any moment, until I was rescued by some men who heard my pleas and came to my rescue."

Eventually we were driven to the top of the Hebgen Dam near the spillway, so that when help arrived, it would be easier to transport the critical patients. I recall waiting outside the trailer where my parents were being cared for when my father called Anne and I into the trailer. When we entered the trailer, we could see our parents lying on a blood-soaked mattress. It was horrifying beyond words to describe what it looked like and to hear my mother cry out, "Please don't let my girls see me like this."

We were quickly ushered outside, but as we were leaving the trailer, our father called out, telling us that our mother was going to die unless we got her help. This upset us to the point where we started crying. We were only twelve years old. What could we possibly do to get them help? We had been through a horrible ordeal ourselves and were without sleep and food. We were covered in blood and gasoline and wore dirty, wet pajamas. Their lives hung in the balance as far as what we could do for them. We were quickly losing hope that things for our family were going to turn out OK.

Help did finally arrive that afternoon; our parents were transported by military helicopter to the West Yellowstone Airport. There they would be transferred to a plane that was being converted to an air ambulance, but unfortunately it was too late. It was such a tragic ending for our family. Mother was just too badly injured to survive. Three days later, on August 20, she died of her injuries in the Deaconess Hospital in Bozeman, Montana.

WEST YELLOWSTONE, Mont.—Sporadic tremors in the Yellowstone National Park area brought fresh concern today about the growing lake behind a mammoth, earthquake-triggered slide in the Madison Valley.

The rising waters threatened two summer resorts and a summer home and increased its pressure on the quake-formed barrier threatening communities down stream where the trapped Madison River once flowed.

Eleven fairly strong shocks and several minor ones were recorded in the area yesterday. A major temblor could cause the huge slide to shift, allowing a deluge to break through.

The body of water, now known as The Lord's Lake, is presently seven miles long and between 70 and 100 feet deep—and it continues to grow. National Guardsmen moved into the area today to prevent possible looting.

DEATH TOLL NINE

The quakes' death toll, meanwhile, reached nine. Mrs. Ray Painter, 42, of Ogden, Utah, died yesterday in a Bozeman, Mont., hospital. She was hurt when the quake split a mountain and sent it thundering down on Rock Creek campground and into the Madison River.

Her husband, who also suffered injuries in the slide, was flown to Ogden today for further medical treatment. He was accompanied by his son, Kenneth.

MRS. RAY PAINTER
Quake's 9th Victim

West Yellowstone, Montana (AP)

A woman injured when a side of a mountain gave way in southwest Montana's earthquake Monday night died today of her injuries. This raised the death toll of known dead to nine.

She was Myrtle Painter, 42, Ogden, Utah. She succumbed to her injuries before noon at the Deaconess Hospital, in Bozeman, Montana.

Mrs. Painter was among the persons injured at Rock Creek campground, where a slide choked the Madison River. She was brought to the hospital by a helicopter and airplane.

It was such a shock losing our beautiful mother. We were devastated and sad to know how badly she was injured and how much she had suffered. The length of time that had elapsed until she could get to a hospital took many hours. We never saw her again after she was taken away by helicopter. No good-byes were exchanged before she died in the hospital in Bozeman. Back in 1959, there were no trauma centers or helicopters that could be sent in minutes to help. Evacuation came slowly, and had to be arranged through the military. Most of the helicopters were far away or on assignment. They had to return to their base for fuel and make preparations for evacuations.

The evacuation time of getting her to the hospital was too long and allowed the infection to become untreatable. She fought so hard to live. Her thoughts, we later learned, were only about her children's welfare. That's who she was! She never thought about herself. She only worked to make life better for those people around her. The smoke jumpers and people that attended to her told us that as badly as she was injured, she never complained.

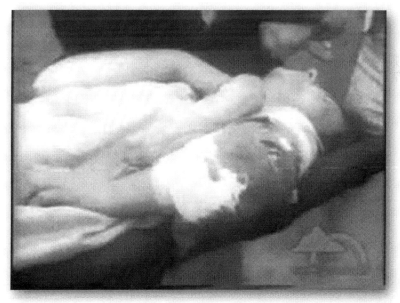

Mother being transported by helicopter

Myrtle Orem Painter was forty-two at the time of her death.

We are keeping her memory alive with stories and pictures. We also have family reunions with remaining family members. It is nice to hear from her friends and family about what a beautiful person she was. I'm sure she would be really happy hearing those wonderful things.

Our mother's name is on the memorial plaque as a reminder of her death, but to our family she lives on. We have a belief and faith that we will someday be reunited with her. This gives us such happiness to know that death isn't the end, that families are eternal.

The Williamses

THE WILLIAMSES WERE a family of five who went on what was meant to be a fun summer vacation together to Yellowstone Park. Instead, the entire family was tragically taken by the earthquake. I get teary-eyed when I think of them, especially when I see their picture. I can't imagine what a terrible shock and loss it was for their family members who love and cherish them.

Robert James Williams (thirty-two), born March 17, 1927, Ashton, Freemont, Idaho.

Parents:
Joseph James Williams, born February 23, 1899, Orleans, Harian, New Brunswick.
Effie May Bainbridge Williams, born 1903, St. Anthony, Idaho.

Siblings:
Mary Mildred Williams, born 1923, Idaho.
Barbara Joanne Williams Skuse, born 1929, Idaho.
Helen Williams Miller, born 1937, Idaho.

Grandparents:
William Daniel Williams, born January 1, 1853, Llanwnnen, Cardiganshire, Wales.
Elizabeth James Williams, born February 11, 1860, Dowlais, Glamorganshire, Wales.

Emigrated from Wales to Liverpool, arriving August 9, 1908, in Boston, Massachusetts on the *SS Cymric.*

Edith (Coy) Williams (thirty), born April 17, 1928, Ririe, Jefferson, Idaho.

Parents:
Russell Oliver McBride, born December 11, 1899, Hyrum, Utah.
Edith Francis Butler, born August 18, 1878, Idaho Falls, Idaho.

Sibling:
Agness McBride, born 1918, Blowout, Bonneville, Idaho.

Grandparents:
William Alvin McBride, born December 8, 1869, Hyrum, Cache, Utah.
Maria Brighamine Danielsen McBride, born September 11, 1877, Soderup, Melose, Holbaek, Denmark. Emigrated September 12, 1904, on the *SS Cedric.*

SS **Cedric**

Great-Grandparents:

Oliver Stephen McBride, born August 29, 1935, Villanova, Chautauqua, New York.

Margret Elmira Sanford, born December 3, 1838, Brown County, Illinois.

Children:

Steven Russell Williams (eleven), born March 26, 1948, Boise, Idaho.

Michael James Williams (seven), born February 11, 1952, Los Angeles, California.

Christy Lyn Williams (three), born January 26, 1956, Blyth, Riverside, California.

* * *

City Family Presumed Lost in Slide
The *Post Register*, August 31, 1959

An anxious two-week vigil by relatives and friends of the R.J. Williams family of Idaho Falls appeared to have ended sorrowfully Monday, although hope has not been completely abandoned that the family may have escaped the fateful earthquake slide in the now memorialized Madison River Canyon in Montana.

Family members were hoping that the Williamses may have had car trouble or run into some unforeseen delay. But the fact that the punctual Williamss did not show up for work at an Idaho Falls store that Monday morning has forced the probability that the family was swept away by the large slide.

The Red Cross Monday still listed the family as "unaccounted for and missing." Two of the children were to have entered school that Monday.

A blue-and-white car is crumpled like a piece of paper at the bottom of the slide (*Montana Standard*).

Monday, August 31, 1959 — The Park-Register,

RELIEVED LOCAL VICTIMS OF EARTHQUAKE

City Family Presumed Lost In Slide

Second Damage Suit

Robert and Edith (Coy) Williams and their three children left on a two-week vacation to the Yellowstone area in their blue-and-white Ford station wagon. They were pulling a rented orange-and-white trailer. The day they left, they had stopped at their grandpa and grandma's house, that of Joe and Effie Williams. That first night they stayed at Staley Springs at Henry's Lake, in West Yellowstone, Montana.

In 2015 I had a chance to talk to Robert's younger sister, Helen Miller, who still lives in St. Anthony, Idaho. She told me what a wonderful little family the Williamses were. She was still so heartbroken. I could tell by talking to her that after all these years, it was pretty painful for her to even speak to me about it. So tragic—I can't even imagine what a shock that had to be to the whole family.

She explained that on the night of the quake, the parents and little three-year-old Christy would have probably slept together in the small trailer. The boys had sleeping bags and were probably settled down for the night inside the car. She said, "On August 17, the family took a trip to Virginia City. This is where the authorities had found they had signed a register at a museum in Virginia City, Montana, late in the afternoon on the day of the earthquake. They hadn't been heard from since then. The family members were hoping maybe they had car problems and had decided to stay in Virginia City." The authorities were fearful that the family, after signing the registry at Virginia City, had driven back to the popular spot at the Rock Creek campground in the Madison River Canyon to spend the night. Robert had told his relatives before leaving that he planned to visit Virginia City and then go to a remote area.

"We Are Going Where You Can't Even Hear the Birds"

The relatives said the two weeks after the earthquake were horrible. Every station wagon that drove by their home was scanned anxiously, and every ring of the phone made the family anxious. They were hoping that it would be the couple, calling to let the family know that they were safe. But unfortunately, that call never came.

Helen told me her brother, Robert, was her guiding light. He always looked after her and told her that he would be there for her throughout her life, so when he died, her world was shattered. She couldn't understand why such a beautiful, loving family would be taken this way.

Helen explained how two weeks after the earthquake, her family went to the slide area in West Yellowstone to search for clothing and camping gear that would indicate the family had been there. Sadly, they didn't find anything belonging to the Williams family. She said it was horrible and unimaginable to see the slide and to know the family was probably buried there.

Robert's family lived in St. Anthony, Idaho, for a period of time. Then they traveled to the northwest with his father, J.J. Williams, who worked for the Bureau of Reclamation.

Helen also told me that the Williams family had moved to Los Angeles, California, when she was six years old in 1942 because her mother had cancer and there was a special radiation treatment that was only available in California. She said, "When Coy was a young girl, she lived with the Williams family. Growing up she was best friends with Robert's sisters, JoAnn and Mary. That is how Coy and Robert met. Coy's mother died when she was a child, so the Williams family became her caregiver."

At the end of World War II, Robert entered the navy, where he served overseas in Japan. After returning from duty, he entered college in Los Angeles, where he studied advertising and salesmanship, receiving a BA. He also started dating Coy, and in 1945, he married Edith Coy McBride in Los Angeles, California, at the Williamses' home. The couple moved back to St. Anthony, Idaho, shortly after their marriage because Robert couldn't find the type of work he preferred. They moved back to Los Angeles, where he worked for a while, and then to Bishop, California, where he was a manager of a Sears Roebuck store. He then transferred to the Sears store in Idaho three years prior to his death.

Helen says the children were adorable. They loved playing outside together and were good students in school. The children attended church with their parents, and they loved sharing time in primary. Steve, who was then eleven, played baseball in the Western Boys Baseball League in Idaho Falls. Christy, who was three years old, was really close to her mother and grandparents.

Robert served as second counselor in the bishopric for the twenty-fifth ward. Edith was the secretary in the Sunday school.

Robert was survived by his parents and three sisters: Mrs. Mary Osborn, of Las Vegas, Nevada; Mrs. Joann Skuse, of Lincoln, Michigan; and Helen Miller, of St. Anthony, Idaho.

Coy was survived by her father, stepmother, and sister, Mrs. Bill Stroschein of Blythe, California.

* * *

An Interview with Joanne Skuse

Aug. 17, 1959, isn't a date the world remembers. But for those who felt the earth shake in the middle of the night and had loved ones perish, it's a date indelible.

Fifty years later, Joanne Skuse, the sister of an Idaho Falls man who died that night with his family, still chokes back emotions when talking about her feelings about it. Her brother, Robert Williams, his wife, Coy, and their children, Steven, eleven, Michael, seven, and Christy, three, perished in the massive landslide triggered by the quake.

The family had camped at Rock Creek Campground on August 17, traveled the day of the quake to Virginia City, Montana, to sightsee, where they signed a guest book register, and then returned to the campground, which was buried just before midnight in the slide.

Williams's sister, of St. Anthony, Idaho, was living in Michigan at the time with her husband, Merle, and their three children.

She didn't feel the earthquake, of course, but she is still feeling its effects. "It's so hard to realize it could possibly have happened," she says. "You relive it, imagining what happened, how much time they had. It can drive you crazy."

She keeps a scrapbook of news clippings and information about the event, but she has decided against attending a memorial service and other commemorations this week on the fiftieth anniversary of the tragedy.

"We decided not to go," she says. Of the twenty-eight people who died as a result of the earthquake, nineteen of the victims remain buried under the eighty tons of mountainside.

Memorial Rites Held for Family
Idaho State Journal, September 16, 1959

Idaho Falls (AP) Memorial services were held here Friday for the five-member Robert J. Williams family, presumed killed in the Madison River Canyon landslide following the August 17 Montana earthquake.

Bishop Virlow Peterson of the 25th ward, Church of Jesus Christ of Latter-day Saints, officiated at the services in the Lincoln ward chapel.

Dedicatory prayer for the family will be given later at the scene of the earthquake slide.

All of the Williams family members are sadly on the memorial plaque. Heartbreaking as it is, I truly believe that they are all together now as a loving, happy family. Someday, all of their losses will be made up. Those family members on earth will one day pass through the veil of this life to the next, where the Williams family is waiting for them.

The Bennetts

Purley "Pud" Richardson Bennett (forty-three), born September 1, 1917, Bliss, Holt, Nebraska.

Irene Bennett, born 1919 in Nebraska.
Irene moved west to the small town of Hope, Idaho, in 1936. She attended school in Hope and graduated in 1938 with a class of seven students. She married Purley Bennett on July 12, 1941, in Coeur d'Alene, Kootenai, Idaho, and they had four children.

Phillip Bennett (sixteen)

Tom Orville Bennett (eleven), born April 2, 1948, Coeur d'Alene, Kootenai, Idaho.

Carole Irene Bennett (seventeen), born January 5, 1942, Coeur d'Alene, Kootenai, Idaho.

Susan Elaine Bennett (six), born October 2, 1953, Coeur d'Alene, Kootenai, Idaho.

Carole, the oldest daughter, was going to start her senior year in high school. Susan, the youngest, was going to start first grade.

4 OF 6 IN FAMILY DEAD—Four of the six members of the F. R. Bennett family, Cœur D'Alene, Ida., were killed in the Montana earthquake. They were camping near West Yellowstone, Mont. Shown in this 1955 photo are, from the left: Bennett; his wife; Tom, 11; Bill, 16, and Carol, 17. Susan, 5, is not shown. Mrs. Bennett and Bill survived with injuries.—Unifax.

Coeur d'Alene (AP)

A mother and her son are the lone survivors of the Bennett family. Purley Bennett and his three children were killed by the Montana earthquake on what was to have been a happy vacation trip. Their pastor says, "They have accepted the tragedy with the most spectacular example of confidence in God that I have ever seen."

O NE OF THE more tragic incidents involved the F.R. Bennett family of Coeur d'Alene, Idaho. Mr. and Mrs. Bennett and their four children, en route to Yellowstone National Park, reached the western end of the Madison River Canyon late in the afternoon of August 17 and decided to spend the night at the Rock Creek campground. Mr. and Mrs. Bennett occupied their house trailer, while the children slept in bedrolls nearby. The Bennetts were awakened by the jiggling of the trailer and wondered what had caused it. Sometime later, Mrs. Bennett recalls she heard a tremendous roar, and she and her husband, alarmed, left the trailer to check on the children.

Suddenly they were struck by a violent blast of air. Mrs. Bennett saw her husband grasp a tree for support. Then, as his feet were swept out from beneath him, he was strung out "like a flag" for a moment before his hold was broken and he was blown away. Before Mrs. Bennett lost consciousness, she recalls seeing one of her children blow past her and a car tumbling along by the air blast.

Her son Phillip was buffeted by the wind and washed downstream by a wave of water. Although his leg was broken, Phillip managed to crawl into a clump of trees, where he burrowed into the mud for warmth and awaited daybreak.

Mrs. Bennett and Phillip, the only survivors, were rescued early next morning and taken to the hospital at Ennis, Montana.

Believed Alone

ENNIS (AP) "I thought I was the only one in the family still alive."

Actually, Mrs. Irene Bennett, thirty-nine, and her son, Phillip, sixteen, of Coeur d'Alene, Idaho, were the only two survivors of an earthquake landslide in the family of six.

Her story was related Wednesday from the Ennis hospital by her brother-in-law, James Burkhart of Hamilton. He quoted her as saying, "But then her son Phil who had also been swept across the river joined her."

Thrown Clear
Billings Gazette, August 20, 1959

"I was thrown clear across the river and I was in the water a long while. When I came to, I was jammed against a tree with a log on my back. I dug myself out of that.

"I thought I was the only one in the family still alive.

"I couldn't walk. When daylight came I saw Phillip and called to him. He raised up over the dirt pile and saw me. He crawled over to where I was to help me."

Phillip, whose leg was broken when he was thrown across the river, managed to swim and crawl back. He has had much scout training and put this to good use. In the darkness he dug a hole and covered himself with dirt for warmth and survived the night.

Just as Phillip and his mother got together in the daylight, they were spotted by other vacationing campers and brought ashore. Killed were her husband, Purley, forty-three, a truck driver, and their children, Carole, seventeen, Tom, eleven, and Susan, six.

Their car and all belongings were washed from shore by a tidal wave created by the quake and landslide.

Irene remarried three years after the quake to John Dunn, her childhood boyfriend, and went on to write a book titled *Out of the Night* about her experience and the process of healing. Phillip grew into manhood and married Robin.

I encourage anyone who would like to know more about this family to get a copy of Irene's book. It is a truly incredible story of survival. To read what Irene and her son Phillip endured during and after the earthquake and how they were able to carry on and rebuild their lives is truly inspiring.

The Boyntons

Bernie L. Boynton, born 1910 in Oklahoma.
He was a vice president at Billings Machine and Welding Shop, Inc.

Parents:
Morton Brightman Boynton, born 1883, Fife Lake, Grand Traverse, Michigan.
Ethel B. Boynton 1891, Indian Territory, Oklahoma.

Siblings:
Morton B. Boynton Jr., born 1912, Oklahoma.
Margaret Anne Greenwalt Boynton Dillon, born 1924, McCurtain, Oklahoma.

Inez Denda Boynton, born 1910, Montana.

Father:
Jacob Denda, born 1870, Herzogovina.

Mother:
Anna Nuyovich, born in Yugoslavia.

Siblings:
Chas, born 1891, Herzogovina.
Selma, born 1900, Austria.
Mike, born 1902, Yugoslavia.
Mickey, born 1909, Montana.

Mary, born 1912, Montana.
Samuel J., born 1914, Montana.
Ralph, born 1916, Montana.

Grandparents:
Albert L. Boynton, born 1837, Cortlandville, Cortland, New York.
Mercy C. Wicks, born 1849, New York.

Daughter:
Marilyn Moes Rickmeyer, born 1940.

AFTER SEARCHING FOR records of the Boyntons for a couple of years, eventually I was able to locate Inez's daughter, Marilyn Rickmeyer, who lives in St. Louis, Missouri. She was nineteen at the time of the earthquake. She had been on a trip to Europe and was to meet up with her parents that next day. Marilyn is widowed and mother to eight children.

* * *

Couple Married in Informal Rites at Church
Billings Gazette, May 22, 1955

Bernie L. Boynton and Mrs. Inez Moes were married Thursday morning by the Rev. E. Paul Cunine at an informal single-ring ceremony in the First Presbyterian Church.

Attending the couple were Mrs. M.B. Boynton, parents of the bridegroom, and Marilyn Moes, daughter of the bride. Mrs. Boynton chose for her wedding a navy blue suit and white accessories. She wore a corsage of white carnations.

Mr. and Mrs. Boynton left immediately after the ceremony for a wedding trip to the west coast. On their return they will make their home at 2532 Longfellow Place, Billings, Mt.

Butte Relatives Seek Record of Boyntons
The *Montana Standard*, August 26

A Butte man and his wife Tuesday asked for information regarding relatives of theirs feared lost in the Madison Canyon earthquake area.

Mr. and Mrs. Pete Miller, Anaconda, Mt., request anyone who saw Mr. and Mrs. B.L. Boynton sometime after Sunday to please contact them. Mrs. Boynton and Mrs. Miller are sisters.

Mrs. Miller said they last heard from the Boyntons at 4:00 p.m. Sunday. The Boyntons were alone on vacation with a trailer rented in Livingston.

"We believe they were in the earthquake vicinity," said Mr. Miller. "They told us that they were headed for the Madison."

Mr. Miller said that somebody may have seen the Boyntons in the Madison area on Monday, the morning after the earthquake. "We would like to know for certain whether they were there," he said.

At the height of the earthquake Monday at 11:37 p.m., (MST) part of an eight-thousand-foot mountain toppled into the Rock Creek campground, at the mouth of the Madison River Canyon. It's believed that some people may have been buried by the slide.

Hunt for Couple of No Avail
Search Party Back from Quake Area

Relatives of Mr. and Mrs. Bernie Boynton held the belief Wednesday the Billings couple are buried under a slide that swept the Madison River Canyon on August 17. A search party returned Wednesday after a fruitless hunt for clues in the quake-shaken area.

The party, made up of Mike Denda, of New York, Mrs. Boynton's brother, Marilyn Moes, Mrs. Boynton's daughter, Mort Boynton Jr., Mr. Boynton's son, Harry Wardell, and Frank Pierce, close family friends, left Billings Monday and returned early Wednesday morning.

The search started at Bozeman, where the group interviewed several slide survivors in a Bozeman hospital. A Mr. Armstrong recalled seeing Mr. Boynton in the fatal slide area. Mr. and Mrs. Clarence Scott, when furnished with a description of the Boynton's car and trailer, were almost positive the Billings couple was parked in the Rock Creek campground in an area known as "The Point" about 4:00 p.m., either Sunday or Monday.

Found Gas Ticket
Billings Gazette, August 27, 1959

Verification that the Boyntons were in the area was obtained from a service station, where records indicated they bought gasoline at 3:00 p.m. Sunday and were headed for the park.

The search moved then to Virginia City, where the group examined clothing and articles gathered from the slide area but found no clues. All of the clothing had been identified by the Red Cross at Bozeman.

With close cooperation from officers and the Red Cross, the party drove to Ennis, where a ranger suggested calling the west entrance to Yellowstone National Park to see if the Boyntons' car had passed through. Making the call, however, the group found that no records of cars or trailers moving into camping areas were kept at the West Yellowstone ranger station.

The next move was an interview of still another survivor, Mrs. P. Bennett, in an Ennis hospital, who could throw no light on the search.

At the slide area in Madison River canyon, the party found another group of articles and clothing gathered from the south of the slide. A close examination of the articles produced no clues.

The search ended at the slide, where a construction foreman sent one man below the slide to check the license number of a blue car stranded below the area. The license number did not check with the Boyntons' number.

Both Pierce and Denda said, "The general slide area was still trembling Tuesday, with small slides occurring almost constantly."

Back in Billings, the only clue left to the group was a rumor picked up that the Boyntons had invited acquaintances for coffee Tuesday morning, August 18. The slide prevented that invitation being carried out.

WEST YELLOWSTONE, Montana (AP)

Two names have been added now to the list of persons missing and presumed dead in Montana's earthquake. This increased the missing to six and brought the probable death toll to thirteen. Nine bodies had been recovered.

Sheriff Donald J. Skerritt, at Bozeman, Montana, placed the names of Bernie L. Boynton and his wife, Inez, of Billings, Mt. on the presumed dead list. Previously they had been listed by the Red Cross as unaccounted for.

Mrs. Inez is the former Inez Denda of Anaconda and is a sister of Mrs. Pete Miller of Butte.

Memorial services were being planned at Billings.

The Strykers

EDGAR H. STRYKER was on this camping trip with his three sons and his wife, Ethel Laverne Stryker, the sons' stepmother, when the couple was lost in a slide at the Cliff Lake campground. Mrs. Stryker had told their neighbor days before leaving on vacation that she was very excited and happy to be spending time with the boys. The boys, Martin, John, and Morgan, were lucky to have survived the tragic slide that took their parents' lives. Alone and afraid, they made their way for help near Ennis, Montana, on the downhill side of the slide. They were reported lost in the quake at first, until they were able to meet up with authorities there and report the tragic death of their parents.

Edgar H. Stryker (thirty-nine), born July 22, 1920, Rochester, Monroe, New York.

Parents:
Dr. Harvey A. Stryker, born July 7, 1889, Newark, Essex, New Jersey.
Grace M. Gramlich, born February 8, 1892, Ohio.

Siblings:
Dr. Clinton Stryker
Mrs. Mayfred Hanks

Grandparents:
Arthur A. Stryker, born 1860, New Jersey.
Minnie S. Reeve, born 1886, New Jersey.

Ethel Lavern Mitchell Stryker (thirty-seven), born 1922, Oklahoma.

Parents:
Pete A. Mitchell, born June 30, 1986, Butler, Kansas.
Priscilla R. Roupp, born August 1887, Missouri.

Sibling:
Georgia Mitchell Gumz, born 1909, Oklahoma.

Grandparents:
Franklin L. Roupp, born January 15, 1857, Illinois.
Martha J. Heard, born 1848, Indiana.

Children:
Martin Frederick Stryker, born January 21, 1944, Contra Costa, California.
John Harvey Stryker, born February 4, 1946, Alameda, California.
Morgan Edgar Stryker, born May 19, 1951, Alameda, California.

The boys were in a tent only a few feet from the tent in which Edgar, their father, and Ethel, his wife, were sleeping. The following newspaper reports tell the story about what happened on that day.

* * *

Ogden Standard Examiner, August 19, 1959

A neighbor, Mrs. James Ghielmetti, said, "Mrs. Stryker had come over last week to tell her about their wonderful fishing trip to West Yellowstone, and how they were looking forward to it. They were wonderful people."

Edgar Stryker's mother was recovering from a near-fatal auto accident while driving to San Mateo, California, at Christmas time. She now had to endure the pain of losing her son and daughter in-law.

By Robert Crennen, West Yellowstone (UPI)
The *Mountain Standard*

One of the graphic stories of the earthquake disaster in this area was recounted Wednesday by a Montana news editor. It was among the countless stories of tragedy and narrow escapes being related by survivors.

He writes Mr. and Mrs. Edward Stryker of San Mateo, California, were killed.

The Strykers were in one tent and the Strykers' three children, Martin, fifteen, John, thirteen, and Morgan, eight, were in another. The family's automobile was in between the tents. Three or four boulders the size of an automobile tumbled of the cliff above. One crushed the automobile and the other crushed the parents' tent. The boys' tent was not touched.

The boys had to hike a half of a mile to Wade Lake to get help.

Son of Mateo Quake Victims Tells Horror
The Times (San Mateo, California), Wednesday, August 19, 1959

Fighting back his tears, fifteen-year-old Martin Stryker today told of how his father and stepmother died suddenly as thousands of tons of rock and dirt thundered down on them in an avalanche touched off by the earthquake that rocked the area near West Yellowstone.

"They couldn't have known what hit them," said the youth, who yesterday was at first was reported missing, as he bravely related details of the tragedy to reporters and sheriff deputies. "I'm glad they never suffered."

Martin said he and his two younger brothers escaped only because their father had pitched a tent about twenty feet way from where his parents had been sleeping in Cliff Lake, Montana.

Story of Horror

The boy said when he and his brothers were suddenly awakened by the tremor, they could hear trees cracking.

"When we got out of the tent, we could see that two trees had fallen across our car and another had crushed our boat."

Then, he continued, a tremendous roar echoed down the walls of the mountain high above their heads as the cascading wall of earth crashed into their parents' tent.

"They couldn't have known what hit them," he tearfully repeated. He said the air was full of dust, making breathing difficult and vision limited. An unidentified camper led the dazed boys to safety. He took them to the sheriff's office in Virginia City, Mt.

The tragedy started on Friday afternoon when the family packed up their car up, and the happy family was off on a two-week vacation. All available space in the car was packed with the camping equipment they expected to need for their annual vacation sojourn.

Left Pet Behind

Arriving at the campsite in the beautiful mountain country located between the two-thousand-foot-high mountain and the river into which the mountain later slid, the family pitched their tents.

The boys, who normally visited their father and stepmother almost every weekend, had brought their pet hamster to go on the vacation trip. But during a hurried family conference it was decided to leave the small animal with neighbors.

In a news bulletin:

Two people died at Cliff Lake campground, fifteen miles southwest of the Madison Canyon landslide, when a large boulder bounced over the picnic table and landed on their tent. Their three sons, sleeping a few feet away, were not injured.

Edgar H. Stryker was on this camping trip with his three sons and his wife Ethel M. Stryker, the sons' stepmother. The sons, Martin, fifteen, John, thirteen, and Morgan, eight, live with their mother (maiden name of Roberts) and spend the summers with their father.

Photo courtesy of U.S. Forest Service

Final Services for Strykers
The Times (San Mateo, California)

Riverside—Funeral services for Mr. and Mrs. Edward Stryker, of Sam Mateo, killed by falling boulders during the Earthquake, in Montana, on August 17th, while they camped along the banks of the Madison River, were announced today.

Rites will be conducted at 12:30 p.m. Monday at the Atheson and Graham Chapel in Riverside. Interment will be in the Mountain View Cemetery, in San Bernardino.

Mr. Stryker was a native of Rochester N.Y. Stryker, thirty-nine, was an industrial engineer with United Airlines at the international airport. He lived in San Mateo for four years and in California since he was a year old.

Mrs. Ethel Stryker, thirty-seven, was a clerk in the attendance office at Hillsdale High School.

He is survived by his three sons, Martin, John, and Morgan of San Mateo; his father, Harvey Stryker; a brother, Dr. Clinton Stryker; and a sister, Mrs. Mayfred Hink, all of Riverside.

In addition to their sons, she is survived by her mother, Mrs. Priscilla Mitchell of Kerman, and a sister, Mrs. Georgia Gumz, also of Kerman.

The newspaper reports tell Martin Stryker's story about what happened to his father and stepmother that night. Edgar and Ethel are no longer just names on a memorial plaque. We now know a little bit more about them. Sons Martin, John, and Morgan thankfully do not appear on the memorial plaque, because they survived the earthquake and mountain landslide.

Margaret Holmes

MARGARET HOLMES WAS on a family vacation in West Yellowstone with her two daughters, Verona and Mary, when the 7.5-magnitude earthquake struck.

Her trailer was ripped apart by the debris from the massive landslide and water. She was thrown out of her trailer and washed downstream, where she was severely injured.

Margaret A. C. Duffey Holmes, born 1888, Meagher, Montana.

Parents:
James H. Duffy, born 1838, Nage, Ireland.
Zadonia Wells, born 1862, Canada.

Siblings:
Charles Duffey, born 1887, Montana.
James Duffey, born 1898, Montana.
May Duffy, born 1890, Montana.
Sadie Duffy, born 1893, Montana.
Martha Duffey, born 1900, Montana.

Daughters:
Helen Marguerite Holmes Schlenz, born 1917, Montana.
Sidonia M. Holmes All, born 1913, Montana.
Germaine Mary Holmes Schreiber, born 1919, Montana.
Verona A. Holmes, born 1914, Melville, Sweet Grass, Montana.

Sons:
Norman I.H. Conway, born 1916, Montana.
Gerald F. Conway, born 1918, Montana.
Lyal W. Conway, born 1920, Montana.

Her husband, John James Holmes, was born in 1886 in Nage, Ireland. Margaret and John were married in 1911 in Harlowton, Meagher, Montana.

* * *

Billings Matron Victim of Quake

Mrs. Margaret Holmes, seventy-two, of 515 Broadwater Ave., was reported Tuesday night to have died in a Bozeman hospital of injuries received in the Hebgen Lake area, during Monday night's devastating earthquake.

With her daughter, Miss Verona Holmes of the same address, she was reported to have left Billings a week ago on a camping trip in the area.

She and her two daughters, Verona, Mary Germaine Schreiber, and Mary's family were camping when the earthquake hit.

Mary Germaine was married to Anton J. Schreiber and they had their daughter Bonnie, age seven, with them on this fateful camping trip. Bonnie was injured as well.

Miss Verona Holmes said she was sleeping in a camp trailer "when I felt something jar me. I yelled, thinking it was a bear.

"Then rocks, brush, mud, and debris caved in around the trailer," she recalled. "I was swept under water for a long way. One leg became entangled between two logs, and I ran and I fell into the river."

Verona states their trailer "was lifted off the ground" and her leg was broken as the earthquake threw her into the river.

One Of Quake Victims

Mrs. Margaret Holmes, 72, of Billings, Mont., is given plasma as she is lifted from Air Force helicopter at West Yellowstone airstrip. Mrs. Holmes, one of first evacuees, died Tuesday night in Deaconess Hospital, Bozeman. She and her daughter, Verona, also injured, were camping in the Madison River canyon when slide hit.

One of the quake victims Mrs. Margaret Holmes, seventy-two, of Billings, Montana, is given plasma as she is lifted from an Air Force helicopter at the West Yellowstone airstrip.

Mrs. Holmes was one of the first evacuees; she died Tuesday night at the Deaconess Hospital in Bozeman, Montana, of injuries she received while camping in the Madison River Canyon when the earthquake hit.

* * *

An Encounter with Bears That Suddenly Became Unearthly Horror

Warren Steele, a Billings, Montana, packing-house worker, was asleep with his wife in their tent in the Rock Creek campground. "The first thing I knew was that the tent was going around, twisting around. I couldn't figure it out. I could only think that a car had hit us, I looked out but I couldn't see a car, but the roar was deafening. There was dust coming off the mountains. Then I saw the whole thing was moving."

Water began pouring through the tent, and Steele and his wife Esther hastily started slogging out into the rapidly rising flood. Esther reached higher ground and safety, but Steele was knocked over by the current. He was carried along, bouncing against rocks and trees. Twice he was hung up on high spots. Each time he was swept off before he could regain his balance. Once his neck was caught in a branch, but a surge of water freed him. He was finally swept ashore, battered and cut but safe.

Mr. and Mrs. Anthony Schreiber and their daughter, Bonnie, seven, friends of the Steeles, were asleep in their trailer nearby when the earth heaved. Mrs. Schreiber's seventy-two-year-old mother, Margaret Holmes, was staying in still another trailer not far away. The Schreibers too thought at first that it was bears. When the landslide came, they were still in the trailer. The wave of water that followed hit them broadside, lifted up the trailer, and swept it along the bank. "I'm positive that we turned over once. I mean over completely, end over end," Schreiber said afterward. "I sure swallowed a lot of water."

Somehow, as the trailer was bouncing along, Anthony Schreiber was hurled out. He managed to hang on, however, and the trailer soon came to rest on high ground. Mrs. Schreiber first boosted Bonnie out through a broken window, and then she climbed out. Bonnie had a gash above her left eye that required thirty stitches to close. Every bit of clothing was ripped off of all of them. They covered themselves with clothing from suitcases they found.

As soon as the Schreibers and Steeles located each other, they began to search for other survivors. They found Mrs. Holmes, who had been swept away by the river. She could walk to higher ground, but the bruising ride through the waters had hurt her terribly.

Margaret may be alone on the monument plaque, but she has a history and a family that loved her dearly.

Memorial Services

Earthquake Memorial Services Thursday August 26, 1959

Helena (AP) Memorial services will be held Thursday afternoon at what may be the final resting place for an unknown number of earthquake victims.

Bishop Chandler Sterling of the Montana Episcopal Diocese said he and ministers from the Catholic and Jewish faiths will conduct the services at 2:00 p.m., probably at the foot of the giant slide, which crashed across Rock Creek campground a week ago Monday night.

Representing the Roman Catholic faiths will be the Rev. Leonard Jensen, pastor at Laurin, near Ennis. Rabbi Max Kert of Butte will conduct the Jewish service.

Service Held for Quake Dead

Ennis, Montana (AP) The souls of those persons presumed buried by the earthquake slide were committed into the hands of God Thursday afternoon from a sun-drenched, windy slope just outside of the Madison Canyon. Nearly fifty persons, including the sheriff's officers, Forest Service employees, and Red Cross personnel, attended the fifteen-minute service, conducted by representatives of Protestant, Catholic, and Hebrew faiths. Six persons at that time were presumed buried by the slide of an eight-thousand-foot mountain, which toppled onto a canyon campground below the night of August 17. The Red Cross has no account of forty other persons that have been reported as missing. Nine bodies have been recovered from the slide area.

The committal rites were held about a mile from the mammoth mile-long and several-hundred-feet-deep slide. Sheriff's officers vetoed a plan on holding the service on the slide itself because it was too dangerous. The slide, however, was visible from the sagebrush-covered slope a mile away.

"These people had come to escape the maddening crowd and found their last resting place in the beauty that they loved." said Rabbi Max Kert of Butte, referring to the pine-covered mountain valley. "From the womb of women to the womb of the earth is but a brief span in days, but the effect of character that is the human soul is of eternity. The anonymity of those sleeping in the ground enhances the brotherhood of those who gathered to bid them farewell."

Services Are Short
Billings Gazette, August 28, 1959

Bishop Chandler Sterling of the Montana Episcopal Diocese recited psalms of the Old Testament. "Unto God's gracious mercy and protection we commit you," he said. "Lord accept these prayers on behalf of thy souls of thy servants departed. Grant them an entrance into the land of life and joy in the fellowship of thy saints."

The Roman Catholic committal services were conducted by the Rev. Lawrence Jensen of Laurin and Father Byrne of Ennis. Assisting the Anglican bishop was Rev. Ralph Krohn of Townsend. Each service took about five minutes.

Rabbi Kert said the ride from Butte to the canyon was the "longest, roughest ride I have ever taken." The minister referred to quake-caused cracks and dips in the road, which produced a wash board effect, forcing a slow drive.

Stories of Survivors

Towering Mountain Flows Like Water into Madison Canyon

AN ARTICLE IN the *Montana Standard* newspaper of August 19 described the slide this way:

In the moonlight, the dirt, rocks, and boulders were like cascading water that was flowing into the Madison Canyon. The awesome pile of debris that came down with the slide stretched across four thousand feet of the canyon floor, with a depth of over three hundred feet. The east fork of the Madison River disappeared beneath an avalanche. A fissure estimated at from thirty to fifty miles long opened up from Hebgen to West Yellowstone. Other campers described the sound as an awful roar. Many thought it was a train, as I did, until we all realized there weren't any trains in the canyon.

Mr. and Mrs. S.B. Gilstand from Helena, Montana were parked about a half mile downstream from the landslide and were among the first to reach the injured. "The roar sounded like the end of the world," Gilstand said. "We were sleeping in our car. It felt as if ten men were jumping up and down on the bumper." Air Force Warrant Victor James, fifty-five, from El Centro, California was parked in his trailer about seventy-five yards from where the main slide hit.

"I heard a terrible rumble and looked up," he said. "I saw the whole damn mountain crumbling. It was awful. I saw a lot of fighting during World War II, but I never heard such a hell of a roar."

UPI correspondent Robert Crennen narrowly missed injury in one of the aftershocks at 8:26 a.m. Pacific Standard Time. It happened near where he, a highway patrolman, Robert Spear, rancher Don Cox, and Sheriff Lloyd Thomas of Beaverhead County were standing. They had just driven to the downstream side of the rock slide. At that point, rocks were still trickling down the mountainside, and two cars could be seen "twisted like a wrung washrag."

"I was just taking a picture when Spear shouted 'Good God, look at that!' There were about five or six huge boulders coming down from the top of the mountain. We were back about fifty feet from the slide. We all jumped in. Spear got the car turned around just as the rocks came crashing down behind us.

"Seconds later, a big ledge broke off the cliff and came tumbling down. One rock made a ten-foot dent in the asphalt highway."

Polsonites Miss Death Narrowly
Deseret News, August 19

Polson, Montana—A Polson resident today told of a "premonition" that probably saved him and his wife from being victims of the massive earthquake-caused landslide on the Madison River.

"It was an act of God, I think that is what is was. The good Lord had his arms around us."

These were the words that were spoken by Tom Greene of Polson as he recounted his escape from the perils of the earthquake Monday night.

Green, a Polson painter, and his wife were vacationing at the Rock Creek camp below Hebgen Dam. They had parked their trailer house and were planning on spending several days at that site.

Green said they had felt uneasy and decided to leave that spot.

"It was a premonition, I am sure," Greene said. "We traveled into Yellowstone Park, spent the day there, and that evening decided to leave for home."

"We traveled over a narrow mountain road through a canyon. There was a thunder and lightning storm. It was raining, and visibility was poor. It wasn't until morning that we realized our miraculous escape. We had been parked right where hundreds of ton s of debris had come down at Rock Creek. The road that we had traveled in the canyon had been closed after the slide."

Arizona Republic, August 19

Mrs. Joseph Henderson Armstrong from Victoria, British Columbia, said the first sign of the earthquake sounded like a plane coming down from overhead.

"I saw a tremendous mass of dirt," Mrs. Armstrong said. "I guess I started to run, and suddenly I was knocked off my feet and I rolled and rolled."

"A second later, I was swept into the water, and then I began to climb over rocks. I thought I had lost my husband and two children, Patricia, eighteen, and Donald, eleven."

"I began to scream my husband's name. Again and again I screamed, and I thought it was no use. Then all of sudden I could hear my husband's voice calling my name. I yelled and asked him if he knew where the children were. And he said they were OK."

"When I got back to Patricia and Donald, they looked like drowned rats."

* * *

"It Was Horrible": Children Were Shouting for Help, Sobbing Quake Survivor Recalls.

Bozeman, Mt. (AP) "It was horrible," an earthquake survivor said today.

Mrs. Clarence Scott of Fresno, California, was one of those camped between the Madison River slide and the Hebgen Dam, Monday night when the earthquakes ripped through the Yellowstone National Park. From her hospital bed in Bozeman, Montana, where she and her husband were taken for treatment of their injuries, Mrs. Scott described to the United Press International what happened to her that terrifying night.

"It was horrible. Children were screaming for help, crying for their mothers. And husbands were begging for their wives to answer," recalled Mrs. Clarence Scott of Fresno, Calif., who came out of the heavily hit Rock Creek area.

That's the way Mrs. Clarence D. Scott described the scene that greeted her when she was thrown out of her house trailer in the area where a landslide, triggered by a violent earthquake, slammed millions of tons of rocks into the Madison River.

At Rock Creek
Deseret News, August 19

"We were camped at Rock Creek, seven miles down from the dam. We were in our house trailer and we were in bed.

"There was a terrific shaking of the trailer, and the television antenna fell off and hit me. There was a huge noise, it sounded like a thousand winds going through the trees. But not a tree was moving at first.

"Then something struck the trailer and pushed it up against a tree. A side and the end of the trailer fell out. And my husband was gone. Then I fell out."

Children Screaming

Someone was screaming for help from someone who could swim. I looked where there had been tents, trailers, and there weren't any. Mrs. Scott explained that she and her husband Clarence had come to Yellowstone for camping and fishing. The place they picked to park their trailer is one of the best and most famous fishing spots in the northwest. It is nationally known to fishermen. Anglers and other campers flock to the area during vacation season and dot the entire valley with their tents.

Sheets of Water

Although Mrs. Scott could not tell it at the time she was thrown from her trailer, a large part of the eight-thousand-foot mountain thundered down into the river. The resulting splash shot sheets of water for hundreds of yards, which probably explains the call for a swimmer that Mrs. Scott reported.

Local Hospital Is Scene of Tragedy as Earthquake Victims Are Cared For
By Annabelle Phillips
Bozeman Daily Chronicle, August 19, 1959

I stood quietly on the stairs and watched the fourteen injured victims being admitted to the hospital here yesterday. An air of hushed sympathy and quiet efficiency hung over the small back entry as one by one the victims were unloaded from ambulances, police cars, and private vehicles by volunteer citizens and hospital personnel.

Shock, fear, utter belief showed in the eyes of some. Many lay with their eyes closed. All were battered, bruised, and bloody. Some had small slips of paper bearing their names pinned to them.

As I watched, I marveled at the speedy efficiency with which the hospital operations were carried out. Within minutes after the victims were taken to the third floor in one elevator, the empty stretchers were brought down in another one. Drivers loaded the equipment and rushed back to the airport for the next group of victims. People, young and old, appeared like magic to offer their services in any way. Blood donors quietly arrived.

Two small boys lingered outside the entrance offering to run errands. I asked them once if more victims had been taken up. Their answer was no lady, just one man, and bottles of human blood. I knew the plasma had arrived from Great Falls. Red Cross women and Gray Ladies arrived to answer scores of phone inquiries and send messages to out-of-town friends and relatives seeking word of their loved ones. People came checking on the identity of patients who bore names identical to theirs.

Relatives of the victims arrived in a surprisingly short time from many areas. Fear was written on their faces. The hospital was on a twenty-four-hour emergency basis. Exhausted nurses and teams of doctors worked on caring for the injured. Disbelief at the magnitude of the tragedy showed in the eyes of one woman as she related her experiences. I could almost see and hear the screams of frantic people searching for loved ones and begging for help.

Terror haunted the face of one shocked woman who saw neighboring campers buried under tons of rock within feet of her family. Close by her side was her uninjured ten-year-old son, offering comfort and reassurance. Uppermost in their minds were word on the whereabouts of his father and sister, who they had expected to find at the hospital. They weren't there.

A small girl was brought in, her head bandaged. The next stretcher bore her injured father. She was probably unaware that the first patient received was her fatally injured grandmother or that her injured aunt was also a patient. Shortly after, the uninjured mother arrived, going from one to the other with words of comfort. I talked in the waiting room to two ladies from Kansas who had just arrived in town from Cody, Wyo., and hearing of the injured had come to the hospital seeking word of their two brothers and their families believed to be camping near Hebgen. They had not been admitted. Tears welled in their eyes as I told them many were believed killed in the area.

As I left after, word arrived that all the injured had been evacuated, and people were still coming, seeking any word of their loved ones.

* * *

Man Who Escaped Death Says Prayer of Salvation
Montana Standard
By John Calcaterra

Ennis, Mt.—"Prayer was our salvation," Melvin Frederick of Elyria, Ohio, said Wednesday in telling how he and his family escaped death at Rock creek campground, which was ripped apart by the earthquake Monday night and the accompanying landslides that night and Tuesday morning. Frederick told how he saw the whole mountainside crash down on the camp area. His story follows.

"We arrived at the south end of the camp about six o'clock Monday night and set up a tent. The place was full. There were about twenty-one people in the immediate area. I know all of them didn't get out. I was afraid there may be as many as fifty people buried in that locality."

Roar Was Tremendous

"I was sleeping with my son Paul, fifteen, and George Whittemore, his cousin, fifteen, in the tent. My wife and daughter, Melva, sixteen, were sleeping in the station wagon. It was about 11:38 p.m. when the quake struck. At first I thought it was a bear tearing through the nearby trees. Someone shouted, 'It's a tornado or an earthquake.' Outside the tent and looking upward, I could see the whole side of the mountain collapse. It looked like a huge waterfall. There was a gush of air, followed by a wave of water from the Madison River."

"My son, Paul, was washed downstream about fifty yards. He was able to get back to the bank but was pinned between two trees and a trailer. Water and mud engulfed him up to his mouth. We were unable to extricate him. I thought he was doomed to death. I prayed hard. There was a miracle, for as we gave one last all-out effort we pulled him loose."

Many Kneeled to Pray

"I had heard my wife and daughter scream. They told me later that they had felt the car in which they were sleeping rollover, but it came to rest on its wheels. One door was all that could be opened. The other was jammed. Someone helped them out of the car, just as it rolled over again. They eventually made their way to high ground, where they and others knelt and prayed."

The Whittemores' boy suffered a severe eye injury and was brought to Butte, MT. Mrs. Frederick and Marva escaped injury. Paul Frederick suffered a serious hand injury that resulted from being pinned between the tree and the trailer.

* * *

More Than One Person Blamed Prowling Bears When Trailers Began to Rock in Earthquake
By Robert Barr

Ennis, Montana (AP)—More than one person blamed prowling bears when their trailers houses began to rock in Monday's earthquake.

Nature quickly set them right. "The bed began to rock and shake," said Mrs. Eugene B. Blair of Stone Mountain, Ga. She was alone in the trailer—her husband had gone to Helena, the state capital, for medical treatment.

"Then I began to hear a roar. It got louder and louder. I thought it was a bear."

"You Do Crazy Things"

"Then water began to come in through the roof. The whole front of the trailer started caving in toward me. The windows broke. Everything inside was tumbling and breaking. You do crazy things at a time like that. I grabbed my car keys and billfold and crawled out the front window."

Mr. Blair's trailer was at Rock Creek campground on the Madison River, where tons of rock fell away from a mountainside. Several campers were killed; others may be buried beneath the slide.

Trees Fall All Around

"Trees were falling all around. Everywhere people were screaming and trying to wade out of the water," Mrs. Blair continued.

"I saw one mother who was lame. Her three children were floating down the river. She was shouting. They finally managed to reach the children and drag them to shore.

"Another man and his wife were chasing their children downstream. The children were floating on air mattresses on which they had been sleeping. The parents finally got them out.

"I tried to get to some people who were camped nearby to see if they were all right. Their car was gone. So were they. I didn't know their names. I never saw them again."

At the rock creek campground, two teachers from Montville, New Jersey, Eleanor Rost and Meg Greenaway, had gone to bed in their car parked just fifteen feet from the river. They had been warned about marauding bears that wander all through the Yellowstone area, seeking food or garbage and frequently giving a playful shove to a parked car or tent during their nightly forays. Like so many others that night, the two teachers were sure they knew what was happening when their car began to lurch violently in the darkness.

"It was like a big bear rocking the cradle," Meg Greenaway recalled later. She leaned over and sleepily flashed the car's headlights to frighten the intruder away. When the rocking continued, she awakened her companion. This was no bear, and whatever it was, it was frightening. They decided to pull out fast.

Before leaving, Med flung open the door to recover a prized iron frying pan, which she had had for years. Suddenly there came a mighty roar from somewhere above them. She slammed the door, and the next thing they knew the car was under water. The tons of debris sliding off the mountain into the river had created a huge wave, which rose above the bank and washed clear over the car.

But the two terrified women started the car and drove to higher ground and safety. As they pulled out they thought they heard screams coming from a tent of teenagers that were camped nearby. The youngsters, reported later, were apparently swept away by the mad waters.

* * *

Wade Lake Story Told

About forty refugees are being cared for in the Ennis Elementary school. Among them was Frank Dodson of Roy, Utah. who was camped at Wade Lake, in the mountains above the river. He, too, thought the first motion of his trailer was caused by a bear.

"Then the trailer started bouncing about three feet off the ground," he said. "I knew then it wasn't a bear. The Dodson children slept peacefully through the quaking moments.

Dodson looked out at the lake, normally placid and calm. "Waves were bouncing straight up, ten feet high," he recalled. "The lake bottom was tossed up onto the banks. Mud, rusty tin cans, bottles, and fish were heaved onto the shore."

At daylight the Dodson walked to nearby Cliff Lake, where Mr. and Mrs. E.H. Stryker of San Mateo, California, had been killed. A rock as large as a truck had rolled over their tent.

First Anniversary of the Yellowstone Earthquake

Many Will Recall Great Madison Earthquake of Year Ago
Montana Standard, August 7, 1960

Residents of many sections of the United States are expected at the earthquake slide on the south side of Ennis, on August 17, when the 38,000-acre Madison River Canyon earthquake area is dedicated. Many of the victims and survivors were from all parts of the nation.

The ceremonies and services will start at 11:00 a.m. atop the earthquake slide. A plaque will be unveiled in memory of those who lost their lives in the landslide. A wreath will be laid at the foot of the huge dolomite monolith, to which the plaque has been attached.

On August 17, 1959, dreams turn to screams—a nightmare in reality. Thunderous rumblings and a rain of boulders came down, haunting the night. In the Madison River Canyon there were twenty-eight people who were dead or dying.

Many turned heroes. Campers—strangers before—helped one another as brothers and sisters.

Survivors clad only in pajamas or anything they could grab to cover themselves huddled together in the darkness. Some sang hymns, some prayed. Dawn came and still no aid. Eventually they rejoiced in the first mercy mission of a helicopter.

It would have taken Uncle Sam, or any other builder millions of dollars, hundreds of men and a couple of years to match the dam that was built in seconds and soon caused the quake lake to form.

* * *

I N 1960, A year after the earthquake, our family was invited to the Madison River Canyon for a memorial service. We did not attend the memorial service, partly because my father was still healing from his injuries. Also, mentally, none of us were able to handle the fear we had of going back to Yellowstone, especially being at the site of the slide. It has taken me a while, approximately thirty-nine years, to finally return back to face my fears. I'm glad I did, because it is helping me heal.

Madison River Canyon Earthquake Area

Gallatin National Forest

Dedication

and Memorial Service

August 17, 1960
11:00 a.m.

THIS MONOLITH IS A PART OF THE HUGE SLIDE CAUSED BY THE EARTHQUAKE OF AUGUST 17, 1959. IT IS DEDICATED TO THE MEMORY OF THE MEN, WOMEN AND CHILDREN WHOSE LIVES WERE LOST AS A RESULT OF THE EARTHQUAKE.

In Memoriam

Sydney D. A. Ballard
Margaret Ballard
Christopher Thomas Ballard
Purley R. Bennett
Tom O. Bennett
Carole Bennett
Susan Bennett
Bernie L. Boynton
Inez Denda Boynton
Merle M. Edgerton, M.D.
Edna Mae Edgerton
Margaret Duffey Holmes
Myrtle L. Painter
Roger C. Provost

Elizabeth Findlay Provost
Richard Provost
David Provost
Thomas Mark Stowe
Marilyn Whitmore Stowe
Edgar H. Stryker
Ethel M. Stryker
Robert James Williams
Edith Cey Williams
Steven Russell Williams
Micheal James Williams
Christy Lyn Williams
Harmon Woods
Erina Maude Woods

Fiftieth Anniversary

I N 2009, THE survivors of the earthquake were invited to come back for the fiftieth anniversary. My husband, Steve, and I did return to Yellowstone for this anniversary. While there, I was able to meet a lot of the survivors of the earthquake and their families. I was also surprised to know that there were other neighboring camps above and around the canyon. Those people had chilling stories of what they heard and experienced that night. Many just wanted to give me a hug for being at Rock Creek campground and the fact that I survived. I was able to meet the smoke jumpers who attended to the injured and thank them for risking their lives and making a difference. I was also able to meet Mildred "Tootie" Green for a second time. I was thrilled to do so because I had always wanted to thank her personally for caring for the injured, especially my parents.

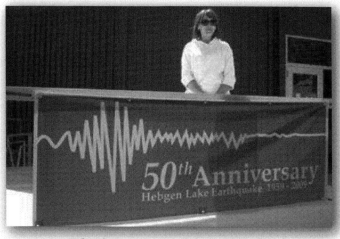

Fiftieth anniversary of the earthquake

On August 15, 2009, visitors were taken on a guided walk to Refuge Point for a reenactment of the rescue that took place the night of the quake.

After the earthquake struck the night of August 17, employees of the Forest Service hurried up the canyon to check for any damage to the Hebgen Dam. They were able to see with flashlights and lanterns that the dam did have some major cracks. They hurried back down the canyon to warn the survivors that they needed to move quickly to a higher ridge for protection, in case the dam broke.

In the meadow of that ridge, now named Refuge Point, is where the smoke jumpers parachuted that early dawn. The men that came to rescue were angels as far as the survivors were concerned. They were the first help that arrived, dropping supplies of food, water, and medical supplies to the stranded campers. In the reenactment, the smoke jumpers again parachuted to the ridge, as they had that night. It brought back a lot of sad memories of that early morning August 18, 1959.

On the night of the quake, survivors were taken to Refuge Point, several miles up the Madison Canyon.

Smoke jumpers at the fiftieth anniversary

Road sign along the drive up the Madison Canyon

After seeing the newly remodeled Earthquake Lake Visitor Center in May 2014, I was really pleased with the results. It has a more open feeling, with many windows to let in the sunshine. It is a beautiful memorial to all who were affected. I love the staff there; they are always warm, welcoming, and kind. I truly appreciate how respectful they are in making the center feel so peaceful.

I didn't realize at the time when I started this project how hard it was going to be. It has been an emotional roller coaster, a very heartbreaking but rewarding journey just the same. I mentioned earlier in my book that I have cried many tears and had many sleepless nights for people I have never met. Every time I came across an article from an eyewitness account, I would get upset, and it would put me back at the campground again. I was always wondering if I saw this family or that family on our afternoon walk that day prior to the quake. My answer is always the same: "I'm sure I did."

This was such a tragic event that changed the lives of so many people forever. It is so sad knowing that nine children didn't get to grow up, attend proms or graduations, marry, or have children of their own. The families came to West Yellowstone for what was to be, a lovely summer vacation. Instead it turned into a tragic ending.

I will say that writing this book has allowed me to meet many wonderful people that I consider friends, especially because we share a common bond. So many tender mercies were given me as I searched for relatives of the victims. In the past two months, one door after another began opening up. Family members I had been searching for and never dreamed of being able to find were now e-mailing me. It's been an amazing experience. When my time comes, I look forward to a great reunion on the other side, and my prayer is to see the face of my lovely mother again and to make up for lost time. Hopefully I will meet the people I have written about and come to love dearly through this tragedy.

GOD BLESS THE TWENTY-EIGHT.

Made in the USA
Columbia, SC
04 October 2021